T0210039

Geechee Gonna Gitcha

Geechee Gonna Gitcha

The FUN-damental Guide to Charleston

By the Child of the Pluff Mud

W. Thomas McQueeney

Library of Congress Control Number:		2018907883
ISBN:	Hardcover	978-1-9845-3959-5
	Softcover	978-1-9845-3960-1
	eBook	978-1-9845-3961-8

To order additional copies of this book, contact:
Xlibris
1-888-795-4274
www.Xlibris.com
Orders@Xlibris.com
772562

DEDICATION

THIS BOOK IS dedicated to the patience of those hosting souls who have welcomed the uninitiated to our fair city. They are the tour guides, the hoteliers, the restaurateurs, the travel coordinators, the merchants, the wedding planners, the wait staffs, the clergy, the bartenders, and especially the public safety officials. They include the "benyas" who are not always Geechee but portray the Geechee sense of living life as happily as it happens.

The Arthur Ravenel, Jr. Bridge at sunset. This
impactful bridge was completed in 2005.
Photo by Author.

ABOUT THE BOOK

GEECHEE GONNA GITCHA is the quintessential welcoming compendium of Everything Charleston written in a most hilarious and entertaining style. It is meant to provide insight, advice, and factual information to assist those moving to the Lowcountry at a rate of nearly fifty people per day as of 2018. The book inspects the culture, cuisine, history, architecture, activities, attractions, and ambiance of America's most historic city. The distinct dialectic language is explored along with the legendary Charleston characters past and present who have elevated its reputation.

The Holy City is a top travel destination. Visitors and newcomers will discover how it's character developed from a one-hundred decline to featured status on the world stage.

Where it matters within the discourse the author shares personal experiences and humorous quotes. This comprehensive exploration of Charleston "old and new" is indispensable.

ABOUT THE AUTHOR

W. THOMAS MCQUEENEY is a native Charlestonian and graduate of The Citadel. He has written seven books in genres to include historical, contemporary, and biographical subjects in addition to literary humor. His Pilgrimages, Passages, and Voyages columns have given rise to his reputation as a Lowcountry humorist. He is self-described as the "Poet of the Pluff Mud."

McQueeney's lifetime of service to others includes board membership to the Medical University of South Carolina Children's Hospital Development Board, the American Cancer Society, the American Heart Association, Our Lady of Mercy Community Outreach, Coastal Council of Explorer Scouts, Patriot's Point Maritime Museum Foundation, Bon Secours St. Francis Hospital, The Hibernian Foundation, The Citadel Brigadier Memorial Fund, The Citadel Foundation, the Charleston Metro Sports Council, and the South Carolina Athletic Hall of Fame.

He has been elected by the South Carolina Legislature to serve on The Citadel Board of Visitors. He served as Chairman of the Medal of Honor Bowl (NCAA Football), and the Southern Conference Basketball Championships. He also chaired the Johnson Hagood Stadium Revitalization Project, a $44.5 million fundraising effort. He is chairman and founder of Santa's Kind Intentions, Inc. He also served as Grand Knight of Knights of Columbus Council 704 and as Chairman of the K of C Turkey Day Run, the largest 5-k race in the state of South Carolina.

McQueeney served as President of the South Carolina Athletic Hall of Fame, is an Honorary Member of The Citadel Athletic Hall of Fame, a recipient of the Southern Conference Distinguished Service Award, and the T. Ashton Phillips Community Service Award. He is married and has four children and four grandchildren. He is a recipient of the Order of the Palmetto, the highest award conferred upon a citizen of the State of South Carolina.

CONTENTS

View of Charleston's High Battery 1952. Not much has changed.
Watercolor by Charlotte Simmons McQueeney.

INTRODUCTION

I T IS A strange attraction. It may already be too late to turn back. It's like a black hole pulling giant stars into its swirl of destiny. And we're just bold enough to call it by other names like *ambiance, culture, character, climate,* and *cuisine.* It really is something else to the Geechees. It's black magic, voodoo, and mysticism. It's bringing others here from afar, as of 2018, at a rate of nearly fifty new residents a day. And they're not even scaling a wall to do it.

The Geechees are gonna gitcha.

Oh, you're wondering: What's a *Geechee*? They are people with their own language that emerged over centuries from a Lowcountry dialect. It's mixed with the lyrical Gullah brogue of African Americans who came here without a choice. It was conjured in that detestable blight of history that left us a vestige of commonality in our inflections, pronunciations, and melodic descriptions. It's a twang with a lilt. It may have ingredients of dialect from the Caribbean, West African, along with the early native coastal tribes of Georgia and South Carolina. The core of the language came from the African American culture and seeped into the entire Lowcountry jargon. To a *cumya*—those who have settled here with book pronunciations from proper upbringings elsewhere—it might be like arriving in Norway. They can't quite understand us, but we understand one another. It was the Geechees who inhabited the old Charleston when there was no one else here but Geechees.

To be sure, Charleston was a nearly unlivable place for a century from 1860 to 1960 *BAC*—before air conditioning!

To a Geechee, there is no singularly affiliated race, religion, or heritage. There are Geechees black and white; Baptist and Jew; Irish, French, Greek, and German. We used to separate ourselves by saying "Geechee-Gullah."

But we became tired of the lengthy explanations. If you're a *benya* (a born and raised Charlestonian), then you're a Geechee. It's akin to having a belly button. Whether it's an innie or an outie, it's still a sign that you were once insulated and isolated.

Geechees are proud. There was once a Geechee who entered a fine Southern college towing his unique pronunciations into the English Department. He insisted that words with one syllable had two, like straight (*stray-it*), and those with two syllables had one, like sheriff (*shurf*). The professors were kind enough to keep him in their department for comic relief. They eventually rooted the Geechee-ness out of him, but it took four years. When presented with his graduation diploma on stage, he said, "Haya go, oot da do-ah." The fella simply fell back upon his convictions. As the satirical poet Samuel Butler stated, "He that complies against his will is of his own opinion still." That Geechee graduate from long ago is writing this book.

This book is focused on capturing the essence of the author's native city across time. It defines a city and its people, both trying to overcome transitional times in a place where the clocks seemed to be broken. The main character is that setting—Charleston, South Carolina. Living here through the 1950's and 1960's was a stark difference to the city seen today. Those decades seemed to be the time when our city woke up and looked out of the window. We were all Geechees then. Our Geechee commonality remains in the Charlestonese inflections—and we're losing it faster than the Wild West lost the bison.

Coming here, one would have no idea of what once was and still is. The chapters will weave through the realities, the mysteries, and the motives. They are arranged without chronology so that random chapters may be read in any order. The intent is to give a cumya or even a stunned tourist the insight to what this city represents.

W. Thomas McQueeney

Charleston single house on Washington Street.
The single house architecture is thematic in the Holy City.
Watercolor by Charlotte Simmons McQueeney.

A CHILD OF THE PLUFF MUD

That oily black upon my tracks
Wherever I trudge in that sludge,
And muck—once stuck on my boots—
Fiddler crabs and sweetgrass roots.
Tis the crime of grime for all time
From the Holy City's pluff mud bay.
It will never ever wash away.

Chalmers Street maintains a cobblestone surface.
Speed limit signs are not necessary!
Photo by author.

ACKNOWLEDGMENTS

T HE AUTHOR ACKNOWLEDGES the extraordinary patience of those in the publishing cycle who awaited a rewrite of several chapters for several months. The rewrites became necessary because much had transpired within the community that would have dated the previously written chapters. Besides, my insomnia was disturbed with pockets of light sleep. You see, at night it seemed to bother me that I had a flow problem. Not that kind of flow, silly. My subjects bounced from the lovely city to my personal experiences and then back again. I was confusing myself! So, I made a list on a yellow pad and divided out the chapters of each.

The separated publications made much more sense. The Xlibris publishing staff has handled the course correction with their customary professionalism.

The book sprang from two ideas conjoined that split like a cell to become two publications. The first plan was to incorporate the foibles of my large and garrulous family into the stream of Charleston's history—especially the last fifty years. When it became apparent that some of the smoother waters of the topic tumbled to rapids, the two boating parties went their separate ways. The family stories were extracted and repositioned with others for a parallel publication, Growing Up Geechee.

Geechee Gonna Gitcha headed out on its own journey. No future search party is anticipated.

With appreciation to Angelie Sage, Nina Arden, Ciara Dixon, Lani Martin, Rica Caro, Lyn Mayers, and Gerri, the submittal was late but laced more tightly. Either my reader or I would have become severely afflicted with literary ADD syndrome under the previous structure. I also wanted to thank my younger brother, Ritchie McQueeney, for reading over several drafts and catching a few chronological errors. I would have sent it to other siblings, but they would fight over who would record the most corrections to shame my intellect the soonest. Besides, if I gave them a draft, there is no way they would spring for a few bucks to buy the book.

Lastly, my lifelong awe of distinctive Charleston art was fostered by my mother, Charlotte Simmons McQueeney (1930-2012). Many of her magnificent productions grace the publication. She was an even more incredible mother of nine children.

It is with a hat-in-hand sense of humility that I present this to you, the reader, who found the Holy City in the heightened level of honor that many before me strived to attain. Many others feel as I do. We earned our humility!

Knights of Columbus Hall 1985.
The author's great-grandfather chaired the building
committee for this structure in 1908.
Watercolor by Charlotte Simmons McQueeney

TITLE ATTRIBUTION

I T IS WITH appreciation that I cite and attribute the title of this book to some unknown person way back when. But I don't know whom to credit. Thirty years ago, I played softball with a group of good friends representing the Knights of Columbus Council no. 704 in Charleston. I played for thirteen seasons—because my teammates were my good friends and there was always a cold beer to enjoy at the end.

Our ragtag softball team traveled to tournaments elsewhere, and our wives would usually accompany us. They came up with a T-shirt with the craziness of "Geechie Gonna Getcha," a forewarning to our softball opponents that this crew from Charleston was prepared to win it all. We never did. But the wives had a great time and sold the "Brand Charleston" to other teams representing Southern cities. They saw us as a band of "Geechies." The spelling of Geechie changed to Geechee because a computer told me I had to do it. Our opponents came to know the odd term as slang for the unique accent of Charlestonians. I use the term throughout this work as an indicative accent of those from Charleston to include what I believe to be the parent language of Geechee—Gullah. That formidable accent has an incredible journey of history.

Though the Knights of Columbus softball experience was memorable, and we did win some local league championships, it was the wives who never lost a game. They called themselves the "Ladies of the Knights." Most of these creative ladies were also Charlestonians. They knew everything we knew—and more. It is to them as a group from years past that I cite the origin of the title to this work.

Rooftops of Charleston. The city's profile is low.
Steeples are easy to find. Photo by author.

CHAPTER 1

Charleston Once Again

W E WERE FOUND before we were lost and then found again. Our city was named for the only dethroned king in the history of the British Empire, Charles I. This stammering, art-collecting monarch was beheaded by the new regime of Oliver Cromwell in 1649.[1] Once the throne was reestablished by Charles II in 1660, our deepwater port had developed a reason for a name. It just hadn't been founded yet. The Lords Proprietors—eight supporters of the new King Charlie—received the land grant. And the first Geechees appeared by 1670. It was just three hundred years before I graduated from high school.

Carolinus is Latin for Charles. But before it became North Carolinus and South Carolinus, they anglicized it to Carolina. The Ashley and the Cooper Rivers formed the slightly relocated Charles Towne (variously shown as "Charles Town"). Yeah, that was named after the decapitated king as well. The two river names both came from Sir Anthony Ashley Cooper, the first Earl of Shaftsbury. There is no Shaftsbury River.

Incidentally, the earl's personal secretary and physician, John Locke, became consequential. His "Fundamental Constitutions for the Government of Carolina" (1669) supported many freedoms including the freedom of religion with the notable exception of freedom to be an atheist. One could not come to Charles Towne and believe in being a non-believer. The Fundamental Constitutions was a brilliant marketing plan. Locke's production also became the template for the United States Constitution![2]

Those who felt oppressed by their beliefs came to the only walled British city in the New World so that it could morph into insular oppression. Oppression had to be a burgeoning issue in the Old World because the nuance of the FCC* got out.

*The FCC back then was known as the Fundamental Constitutions of Carolina. It was the world's first initialism, certainly invented in Charleston.

Before the Hari Krishnas got to the airport, the Quakers arrived. Oatmeal was not near as popular before Quaker Oats. They came to Charleston and left ten years later because the sailor population of the city needed too many pubs and other enticements. The Society of Friends headed on up to Pennsylvania, but their membership has been drifting back to our bars on East Bay Street over the last few years. East Bay Street used to be called E. Bay. But some dot-com capitalist had an epiphany in a drinking establishment there one night and stole away our good street name. They don't sell epiphany there anymore.

Most of the other original faiths stayed—the Lutherans, the Methodists, the Greek Orthodox, the Calvinists, and the Jews. Charleston has the oldest of many of these congregations in the entire South. The Jewish population grew to become the second largest in America outside New York. The Baptist religion was original to Maine, but the Southern Baptist Convention originated in Charleston. If you see any of them in the East Bay Street establishments, buy them an epiphany.

You might wonder—What is a French Huguenot? They certainly did not need the modifier of being French. Huguenots had no other nationality back then. The Huguenots are a Protestant Reformation sect of France, much like the Lutherans of Germany or the Calvinists of Switzerland. The French Huguenot Society is the oldest of its type in America. In fact, it is the only one in America. They have their own beautiful Gothic church with a catchy name. They call it the French Huguenot Church—again, the only one in America![3] Some of the old Charleston names are of Huguenot origin, including Manigault, Huger, Poinsett, St. Julien, and Ravenel.

All of these newcomers arrived to coexist with the native Kiawah Indians, the hungry alligators, and the experience of a sweltering Charleston August. Imagine being here before ice-cold beer, hominy grits, and Deep Woods <u>Off</u>!

My maternal progenitors waited forty years before all was clear and then came on over to cast their lot in America. They did a lot of casting because I'm still running into distant cousins on my mother's side I never knew existed. I did a "23andMe DNA" test a few years ago, and my report page cites another fifteen or twenty relatives within the closer cousin range about once a month. I can't get any one of them to lend me a few bucks until payday. They're scattered all over Charleston like ants at a picnic.

Over the next seven score years, the thriving port brought in enough well-funded rabble-rousers to decide that prosperity was too prosperous. It was nice here in 1860. Then somebody said, "Hey, let's start a war. But let's not kill anybody." So, on the morning of April 12, 1861, the hoop-skirted Geechee women turned out at White Point Gardens to watch a war begin. Looking back, it was a bad idea. The newly uniformed CSA Army fired on Fort Sumter for thirty-four hours. The occupiers surrendered and were given permission to sail away. Nobody died, except a Confederate soldier who misfired a salute cannon as the occupiers sailed away. Indeed, the war had started.

By August 1863, the 567-day Union bombardment of Charleston had begun. It was the most protracted siege of a city in world history, ending just weeks before the war's end in 1865.[4] The most financially successful city in America was reduced to mostly rubble. The rabble-rousers became the rubble-raisers.

The war was a hard-fought conflict of many ideals, institutions, and intolerances. Team South finished second in the league standings. We lost the war but still had the sunshine, the ocean breezes, and a deep port. It would take more than a hundred years for those constants to matter again.

In what I would call the "enduring century" (1860-1960), Charleston became one of the most devastated places in America. Besides a vacant economy, we managed to bring in a few health epidemics, a few more fires, a major earthquake, and too many hurricanes to count. The hundred-year decline defeated many but emboldened others. The proud stayed with a deep-seated belief that Charleston would again become what it once was. They would eventually find the high ground. By 2009, this battered city became the number 1 Travel Destination in the world according to Conde Nast Traveler magazine. You can find the old issues at any realtor's office waiting room.

The relevance of the cultural history of "Charleston Past" can be seen in the attire, disposition, and insight of those encountered within the Charleston community presently—in the middle of our fourth century. Yet that true born-and-bred Charlestonian is now the minority—diminished to about 15 percent of the 2018 population. The Geechee tide has turned. We are the fiddlers among the blue crabs.

In so many fortunate ways, the assimilation of the races in Charleston has dramatically affected the benevolent culture of the city. A war that tore apart a country found two peoples with a common thread. They honored the land. It was the land that provided shelter and sustenance. It was the land that truly mattered. The Lowcountry was devastated, but the land was the land—and it was fertile.

Having a pedigree in Charleston would have been beneficial. But this became a place where the genteel of society couldn't even get a pedicure while perched on a pedestal. In our case, the McQueeney pedigree was vague and loosely substantiated as information that should remain undiscovered. Somewhere way back when, it became likely that the Irish McQueeneys arrived in Charleston despite suspicions of equine appropriations (horse thievery) and being mercenary paramours. That's just an uneducated guess because an educated guess would inevitably turn up worse.

Prior to the War Between the States, the city's high society found a home in the port city. Wealthy rice plantations supported the generations. It seemed that a new society was born each season. Charleston has several societies that stayed the course and closed their membership lists for decades at a time. However, some societies fell by the wayside.

The Philomathean Society died off a century ago but did attract gentlemen to debate the critical matters of the day.[5] They met at Stoll's Alley, not too far from what was once Charleston's red light district. We dare not assume a connection. No one is sure what happened to the Philomatheans. They did not move to Philodelphia.

The Charleston Ugly Club met at Williams Tavern and hurled eloquent insults at one another.[6] They promoted their odd greeting with charm:

> *Ugly mortals, hither haste,*
> *Enjoy our mirth, enjoy our feast,*
> *Bring noses crooked, noses hooked,*
> *Noses swollen, noses crooked,*
> *But each must bring an honest heart,*
> *Or bear this sentence—hence depart.[7]*

The Charleston Uglies formed shortly after the American Revolution but must have run out of insults and disbanded. The higher likelihood is that the members all got married and were able to get their insults hurled to and fro at home.

The aristocratic side of my family has filtered the information that the most proper societies accepted us. These were probably frequented by my maternal pre-Revolutionary family. My grandfather was a member of the St. Cecilia Society, named for the patron saint of music. This elegant old society had a magnificent building on Broad Street until the Great Charleston Fire of 1861. The St. Cecilia's Ball hosted the highest of high Charleston gentry. The society was founded in the 1760s and staged concerts.[8] But the St. Cecilia Society is not even the oldest of Charleston's still-flourishing societies. The South Carolina Society began in 1737 and the St. Andrew's Society began in 1748.[9] Yes, they pre-date the United States. It could be that my maternal family ancestry was in town but never received the invitations. Family records show that we arrived in the 1720s. That makes me a "blueblood Geechee!" I should have been invited to many more debutante balls. But I wasn't!

The paternal side was more egalitarian. My father joined the Hibernian Society and the Knights of Columbus, ostensibly to find a place for a cold beer and some quiet time. His legacy commitment to two buildings with a backbar assisted both me and my brethren to be accepted in bars all over town. I have qualified for honorary lifetime membership in both organizations but get no discounts on the beer. The latter is a benevolent Catholic Men's organization. When I served as its Grand Knight (1985—86), it was still an all-white council. Founded in 1908, I would need willing minorities and a timely opportunity to change the culture. Fortunately, both happened. It was crazy, especially, that any religiously affiliated organization was segregated into the mid-1980s.

The Hibernian Society is the oldest benevolent Irish society in America. Its Greek revival hall on Meeting Street is an iconic architectural mainstay of the city. Typical of many old Charleston societies, their membership waiting list is nearly fifteen years. Fifteen of the last eighteen mayors of Charleston have been Hibernian Society members—perhaps a statistical anomaly.

I have had the great honor of speaking at banquets and other functions extolling the benefit of the old Charleston Societies. One would surmise that they are losing their importance and standing. Not so. They are more popular than ever. They have touched every segment of society—men, women, minorities, religions, and nationalities. My theory is that they must continue to bring the community together because all of society is being attacked by another demon—social media. Facebook, Twitter, LinkedIn, and Instagram have ridden in as the four horsemen of the digital apocalypse. Now, if you can't spell apocalypse, it's not the end of the world!

Young people cite hundreds of "friends" that they have never met because of social media. I make the case that friends are those that you may know better by their laugh, their handshake, their mannerisms, and through eye contact. Societies provide that reality.

A smartphone may give one directions via GPS, a photo catalog, stock quotes, email, the time, and sundry other advancements. But they interrupt conversations, disrupt church services, and take needed personal interaction time away from everyone. They have a time and a place that should not impede interpersonal relationships. Societies breed profound interpersonal friendships that last a lifetime.

What is at risk are dignity and decency. The courtesies of greetings and the heartfelt participation in the needs of others that societies provide cannot be underestimated. One cannot find an old society in Charleston without a meaningful contribution to the benefit of the entire community.

If you ever get invited to one, do not bring your smartphone!

Though the aforementioned waves of immigration have found their respective niches in the many honored societies of Charleston, there can be no mistake that the most considerable lasting impact upon Charleston's society is indelibly and importantly African.

The city that stands today is ostensibly the city that Africans built. The "Gullah" tone in the Charleston dialectic pronunciations is most influenced by the African inflection that originated in Angola. We Geechees are its shadow. The rich and delectable Charleston cuisine has rudiments in the Ivory Coast, Surinam, and Colonial West Africa. We know these tastes in our poultry, our sauces, our fresh seafood, and our "hominy" grits. Often overlooked, the total impact of the African influence on Charleston may be inestimable. The influence of African American culture has become more identified in the last thirty to forty years. Kwanzaa is a cultural community festival celebrated the week after Christmas. The MOJA Arts Festival has gained broad community support for African art. These worthwhile events showcase both the traditions and the heartbeat of Charleston's burgeoning African American community.

Yes, there is something special to be found in the Holy City. It could be something every cumya is seeking, and every benya exudes. It is the hospitality of home in the open-armed invitation to stay and enjoy. It is here for all of us.

By now, the terms of benya (has been here), and cumya (has come here) have revealed their Geechee-secret designation. There is only one other category of person to be described—an O'Blivy (those oblivious to the discovery of paradise on earth). We can only pray for those poor souls.

Charleston is a proud city—too proud not to persevere. This is a happy city as well— laughter contorted in the face of disaster. And it is an enduring city—a lineage of humility, civility, and servitude. It is the city of unavoidable Geechees, and they are determined that they will win you over. It is why we exist. Geechees are gonna gitcha!

Catfish Row on Church Street (DuBose Heyward
background for Porgy and Bess).
Watercolor by Charlotte Simmons McQueeney.

CHAPTER 2

Charleston Geechee Terms

I GREW UP in a home where my mother called my father "Bully." His given name was Billy. He had always been Billy. But my Geechee mother could not pronounce her husband's name. For the rest of his life, his friends and family called him what my mother mispronounced—Bully. That's not so unusual in Charleston.

My momma's Geechee was thicker than my daddy's Geechee because my Charleston-born father was a first-generation American. My mother earned her Geechee-ness from over three hundred years of ancestral verbal domestication in the Holy City. We knew her common words like hawses (horses), rivvuh (river), and cahn (corn). She grew up between the two rivers— the Ashley and the Cupah (Cooper). She could not hep but to leave the L out of "help." She pronounced two syllables in door (do-wa) and boat (bo-at). Mom liked the word col-yum better than saying "column."

My Geechee mother used to ask if I'd pick up abode at da lumba sto for her. She wanted to replace some decking. She could do that well. She had her own hamma, nay-els, and she even owned a chay-en saw. Her sister, my aunt, must've enjoyed gardening because she had an affinity for a patick-u-lilly. It was her way of pronouncing "particularly." I have siblings that say choose-dy for Tuesday. Sometimes I can't even understand my siblings.

The Lowcountry vernacular dictates that any word that has "ou" sounds comes out as "oo." "House," "about," and "out" can be introduced to newcomers as hoose, aboot, and oot. Four years of studying in The Citadel's vaunted English Department nearly cured me. I slip up every now and a-gin.

When I was a young reader of the sports section in our local newspaper, I would thumb over to another section just to read a great Charleston columnist. This cumya writer entertained all of Charleston with his brilliant humor. The Doing the Charleston feature column was the brainchild of Frank Gilbreth, who also authored the best-selling book, Cheaper by the Dozen. He wrote for the Charleston News and

Courier, which he "Gullah-fied" as the "Noose and Korea." His keen ear caught the accent well. Here's his partial list:

Lack: Enjoy, i.e., "I lack fried chicken."

Poet: To transfer liquid, i.e., "Poet from the pitcher to the glass."

Play-it: Something to eat grits off of.

Snow: To breathe loudly and heavily while sleeping.

Dearth: The world we live in

Wheel: The kind of mammal Moby Dick was.

Year: Listen.[10]

We like acronyms, too. Sawbs is a tricky one. It's SOBs. But not those SOBs. In Charleston, that means someone who lives South-of-Broad-Street. Those SOBs are in the high rent district. It's like owning both Boardwalk and Park Place on a Monopoly board. The SOBs talk like other Geechees, but they do it from more square footage.

We had to learn to laugh at ourselves long ago. Someone here invented SNOBs, too. These are the Slightly North of Broad Street folks. A fine restaurant has that moniker. We even have SLOBs. Summer Lovers of Beaches.

Over the years, pundits have added hundreds of common words that have been attributed to Charlestonese, Gullah, or Geechee. We're not guilty of all that they charge us. Some of those words come from Atlanta and New Orleans. All of our colloquialisms should be excused as accepted regional Geechee mispronunciations we promulgate (we sez em alot). They make the trip to Charleston more interesting for the uninitiated.

A few of my favorites include innit, which could be "Isn't it'" if mis-stated correctly. Innit so? Innit can be substituted with iddin. Iddin it so? "Bald" is a word that goes with peanuts or shrimp (shremps) down this way. They're both meant to be warm and soft. Y'all is our word and y'all need to get used to it. We have let other Southerners borry it. And whoever said that ain't ain't a word ain't from yuh (here). Here, the female offspring is the dawtuh and the second month is fibbyweary.

I had an old Charleston friend who couldn't say "children." He said, chillens. Sometimes you hear the same mispronunciation as chirren. Endearing word!

Johnny Wooden was a legendary basketball coach at UCLA. But here, Johnny wooden share iz cupa watah should be self-explanatory.

The waiter may bring the muzzard (mustard), main-A's (mayonnaise) or the cait shup (ketchup) for your sam wishes (sandwiches). Didja want anudduh Coke? Or yahatanuf?"

We have even changed names of places with our Geechee-ness. What was properly Mathews Ferry Road became Mathis Ferry Road. Coastal destinations like Debordieu became debby-doo and Wadmalaw became *watta-ma-law*. DeBordieu is a lovely French name that comes from *D'abord Dieu*, or "borderland of God." Ya just can't argue with that.

And just wait until you hear our idioms. There are simple expressions here that everyone knows. Praysbygawd is "Praise be to God." Hayazakeit means drunk. Uddadablu means suddenly. Peydipypa could mean face the consequences or to send a check for your newspaper subscription. Taikyapic.

You'll hear hundreds of words and expressions that you may not understand. Ask the Geechee nearest you. The answer may be funnier than the terminology about which you inquired! Or maybe you should just listen for a while and be patient. Most cumyas will figure out what a Geechee means within a minute or so.

The Sebring-Aimar House was built in 1836. Watercolor
by Charlotte Simmons McQueeney 1961.

The horse carriage alleyways remain a hidden part of the old city. The way it is remains as the way it was! Photo by author.

CHAPTER 3

The Kiawah and the Cannibals

THE FOLKS THAT came over in 1670 on a ship appropriately named The Adventure saw someone moving in the bushes. It was probably an authentic Native American. Some fool who couldn't count longitudes called them Indians. We'll be non-politically-correct and go with that moniker for now. It would surprise most to know that there were as many as nineteen Indian tribes scattered around what is now Charleston.

The most notable of these were the Kiawah. They hunted, fished, and left piles of oyster shells at what we now call White Point Gardens. That's how it got its name. The Kiawahs were friendly. They seemed to like the new golfers coming in to play on The Ocean Course. But that was later. The new Kiawahs are retired CEOs, movie stars, and sports celebrities.

There were other names like the Catawba, the Santee, the Westo, and the Chicora. The easy-to-pronounce names stuck. The hard ones flittered away.

The first European-Charlestonians were relatively unconcerned about the surrounding Indians, though they eventually built a wall. The real threat was the Spanish. The French were not far behind. When Charleston was settled, there were no permissions granted from either of these other powerful foreign governments. The Dutch never got involved because they already had plenty of lands susceptible to high tides.

It was the Kiawah cassique (chieftain) who pointed to a site up the Ashley River that would be safe from the Spanish. They had seen the Spanish come to the Carolina coast in years past. After ten years (in 1680), the settlers moved to the peninsula because they felt it could be better strategically defended—not from the Indians, but from the dreaded Spanish.

As point-of-fact, the very first named hurricane in America was named in Charleston as the Spanish Repulse Hurricane of 1686. Charlestonians were tipped off by the tribes that a large Spanish force was coming to destroy the young English colony. But the hurricane changed history. Two Spanish warships grounded into the shore and the commanding general drowned.[11] Crisis averted!

It was fortunate that the colony found peace with the natives. For our European role, we helped the Kiawah with their crops and taught them many nuances that came from merry Old England. They taught us to eat oysters in months that had Rs (from September to April). It's a good rule. Never eat an oyster in Augarst!

Unbeknownst to them or us, the merger of the civilizations was devastating. We carried diseases that they had not experienced and for which they had no tolerance. Many died as a result. This unintended consequence was a significant blight upon the settlement of the New World.

The trades within the cultures did prove beneficial. Much of the European refinement assisted the surrounding tribes. There were better construction methods, better metals and other materials, and better ways to prepare foods.

It's worth noting that the Westo tribe was considered cannibals and was a threat to the Kiawah. The English settlement was a protector of the Kiawah. Other tribes found the new English colony at Charles Towne Landing to be a benefit, as well. The settlement enjoyed the fortune of the Kiawah and several other tribes ready to come to their defense. Early Charles Towne persevered.

So, what happened to the Kiawah Indians? In time they traded land on the peninsula for other lands away from the traffic. Where'd they go? To Kiawah Island. They had the best island on the coast. But their numbers dwindled. In time they moved further inland to the Combahee River. Within a hundred years there were very few Kiawah Indians left. If nobody else stands up to take the blame, I will. My ancestors on my mother's side came to Charleston when the Kiawah nation was still going strong. By generational authority, I blame us.

And the Westo? They died off, too. When cannibalism is a rumor, the campfires eventually burn out.

Sunset over the Holy City's low profile. The
Geechees are known to come out at night.
Photo by author.

CHAPTER 4

The Confluence and Influence of the Waters

B Y NOW YOU have been told a handful of times that the Cooper River and the Ashley River come together at Charleston to form the Atlantic Ocean. Actually, they constitute Charleston Harbor first. The Cooper River comes from back up a ways into Berkeley County and joins with the Wando River just before the harbor.

The Ashley River became the reason for those magnificent plantations that tourists visit from across the world. That garden district is the favorite of horticulturalists everywhere. All of these exquisite and preserved properties are on Ashley River Road. The state highway department put a number on the road so that mapmakers could fit it in little tiny shields. It's State Highway 61. You can drive it at night with no lights on if there's a full moon. Just look up and stay between the live oak canopies. To be fair, I haven't done it in years.

Start out at Drayton Hall. Here you'll see the earliest and best Palladian architecture in the United States. They say that the mansion has never been restored. Maybe not, but it has been swept and dusted often enough. It is preserved meticulously. The original paneled woodwork and carving details are stunning. The grounds are lovely, as well.

The formal gardens at Middleton Place are best seen in the spring, summer, and fall. The estate home is a separate tour with portraits, jewelry, and distinctive furnishings. The plantation house appears bigger inside than it is outside though it has no basement. Maybe it's an illusion. Be careful where you walk near the horse stables. There are water buffalo, pigs, sheep, and an assortment of birds that do not fly (peacocks, roosters, hens, and Southern girls with parasols). Do not feed the alligators. And never sit on the riverbank at night.

Magnolia Plantation and Gardens is four miles back toward Charleston. It was established in 1676 and opened to tours in 1870. By many accounts, it is considered the most beautiful gardens in the United States. There are settings at Magnolia Gardens that beg for photos. The Magnolia Gardens Kodak film sales have dropped over the last few years, but they have made it up with other attractions like a petting zoo and a boat ride. Read the advice in all of the travel magazines. They love the place. Those magazines have top journalists and photographers with discounts on the leftover Kodak film.

The Cooper River and the Wando River have plantations as well, like Boone Hall, Mulberry, and Brickyard. Boone Hall Plantation is an exceptional choice for a Lowcountry destination wedding. Finding a suitable bride for an unsuitable groom is always the conundrum.

Near Charleston are other serpentine waterways of interest. The ACE Basin is an acronym for the Ashepoo, Combahee, and Edisto Rivers. It is considered the most unspoiled (read: pristine) estuary system on the East Coast. It is largely undeveloped. All three rivers empty into St. Helena Sound. Most of the conservation land is one county over from Charleston (Colleton County). It is easy to take your mind back 350 years to see what the first settlers encountered at the coast. The natural habitats for sea and land birds conjoin. One can see eagles, pelicans, and ospreys within the same horizon view.

The Stono River is part of the Intracoastal Waterway. It's wide, but it has sandbars that can be seen at low tide. I used to live on the Stono River and was amazed at the amount of commercial barge traffic moving to and fro. Like most of the rivers in South Carolina, the Stono is clean and natural. I've seen deer swimming in it, so I did too. Before Wappoo Cut was engineered, the old plantation crops made a big turn up the Folly River to get to the port in Charleston. Wappoo Cut became a deepening of a creek that shortened that river trip. It was completed in the 1700s. Do not swim in the Wappoo Cut. The current there is unmanageable. The home sites, especially on the James Island side of the Cut, are spectacular. They are perched on one of Charleston's rare bluffs. Our definition of a bluff is shorter than anyone else's definition across the globe. We're talking maybe fifteen feet. Mount Pleasant has no mountain and likely rises to the spectacular height of twelve feet at the Old Village. That's it. Never be confused by our topographical names.

Our beaches are lauded as among the cleanest and best in the southeast because that's what they are. The issue that has been a constant is beach parking. Because the beaches are residential and access points are laid out methodically, finding suitable parking is difficult. At Kiawah Island, Beachwalker Park solves much of the need. But get there early. The park is operated by Charleston County Parks and Recreation. There are many amenities including dressing rooms and grills.

The Isle of Palms has a similar situation but smaller. There is insufficient public parking outside of the Charleston County Park area. However, the water temperature and the sunshine are comparable with the other Charleston area beaches. But you knew that. Nearby Sullivan's Island has crowded restaurants all summer and most of the winter. Parking is scarce. However, about twenty thousand people make their way to the Polar Bear Swim every January 1st sponsored by a local pub. I have attended this free-spirited outdoor asylum. The water temperature on January 1st is down to about fifty-five degrees. Nobody stays too long.

Folly Beach is a special place. I nearly drowned there in an undertow when I was eight. But I hold no grudge. I made it out to the shore and have since learned to swim. The island is long and narrow and has neat old houses from the early 1900s interspersed with newer additions. They have a massive commercial pier and a pavilion. There are unique restaurants and surf shops. Surfers love the "washout" where Folly becomes two islands at high tide. Just off the east end is the Morris Island Lighthouse. It was built in 1877 when it was on land, but erosion took it to sea. Restoration efforts are ongoing.

If you're really adventuresome, spend the weekend down at Edisto Beach. It even has a campground. The drive out that way is pastoral and calming. The beach area has more homes from the 1950s and 1960s along with a lagoon, a backside inlet, and a golf course. The locals wouldn't want me telling you about the fantastic experience of visiting Edisto Beach because they want to keep it small and neighborly. So, don't tell anyone there where you heard about Edisto.

Geechees are often asked deep and profound questions by the cumyas, like "Which beach is closest to the ocean?" That takes some considerable cogitation. The best reply from our uniform sense of welcoming is to present the sincerity of our Geechee smile with the universal answer, "It depends on how far your umbrella is from the sand dunes."

The waters allow the land its livability. Water is a most plentiful resource. It moves lazily past us, rolls in on the tides, and sprays a refreshing taunt when the heat dominates. It can rise from the harbor or sting us in the most violent of storms. Water scares us more than the wind in the approach of a hurricane. But it is the water that sustains the Geechee and turns our focal peninsula into Eden.

Drawing of Old Charleston Museum (demolished 1981).
The museum hosted a children's program in the 1950s—Nature Trails.
Pencil rendering by Charlotte Simmons McQueeney.

CHAPTER 5

A Diminishing Breed

THE CENSUS FOR Charleston in 1890 placed the city of Charleston as the fourth largest in all of America. The 1860 census, before that "recent unpleasantness," placed Charleston as the South's second largest city, only behind New Orleans.[12] The year 1861 changed everything.

That steep decline lasted a full century despite the progress of mankind elsewhere.

So, what has changed that? Should we native Charlestonians boast? Well, to an extent, sure! We stayed. We survived. We endured. But the positive progress that Charleston has enjoyed owes a significant debt to the cumyas—those that came here and merged into our culture. Ahem! That may not go over well with my brethren and sisteren.

If you're not from Charleston, but live here now, you are the overwhelming majority. Nearly 85 percent of all Charlestonians today were not born here! So, by deduction, it was that 85 percent that changed us with new ideas, infusion of perspective, and adaptive sensibilities. They brought other industry and technology. They broadened our culture, and they helped us to upgrade our infrastructure. Embrace them! They helped us to rise again!

Take heart. We still have our shrimp 'n grits and our she-crab soup. And though we all seem to know one another; our overwhelming native attitude is one of welcome. Those silly folks that go around saying, "If'n ya don't lakit hayah, hedon beck" live in Ladson and Meggett. We don't pay 'em no never mind. Take no offense.

After all, when the extended map reads lovely names like Goose Creek, Folly, and Hell Hole Swamp, it's gotta be colorful.

Every time we check the latest figures on the growth of the Metro Charleston area—on the approach side of 800,000—we get a new figure of how many move here daily. For the record, when they report "new residents," they are counting babies whether they are yours, mine, or ours. That's at a pace of eleven per day. Together with the move-ins, also new residents, we bring in forty-five per day (as of 2018).[13]

The braggadocio is a bit of a stretch. The growth is here, but it is nowhere where we proud Charlestonians think it is when placed within a national perspective. We've grown to the seventy-fourth largest[14] metropolitan area in the U.S. Remember, we were once fourth! We are growing at a rate that is twenty-fourth fastest in the country.[15] No big deal—unless you're planning infrastructure needs.

Native-born Charlestonians are indeed a diminishing breed. And you can't just recognize their presence by the sight of a slack jaw or baggy pants. You have to get them to talk. That's when the Geechee comes out. It is their unmistakable mark of authenticity.

View to the harbor from Mount Pleasant.
Taken from Governor James B. Edwards' back
porch (with his permission, of course).
Photo by author.

CHAPTER 6

Bats, Bugs, and Bait

IN CHARLESTON, A cut-up chicken neck is blue crab bait, but only for the wealthy. The Geechees might find a stew for such an excellent cut of meat. Shrimp bait is cornmeal. But this chapter is not about bait. The bait was used to get you to read about the bats and the bugs.

Like other parts of the country, we get our share of mosquitoes, deer flies, and wasps. With anticipation, many precautions can eliminate much of the concern that they will ruin our gentle evenings. We have the sprays, ointments, and lotions. We are no worse or no better than anywhere else. And we will not brag about having these pests among us because it's like bragging that we have to pony up taxes on April 15. It's a universal truth.

The bug world, though, may be slightly different here. We have carefully chosen names for our Geechee bugs. In the late spring, it is not unusual to itch and look nutty slapping at bugs that just ain't there. We call those little critters no-see-ums. Cute name. They really exist. Their name describes them to the average observer but does not precisely explain what they do. They wreak havoc. They raise golf scores, they ruin lake fishing, and they crash the family picnic. They have been known to close down whole nudist colonies.

By Geechee calculations, the average no-see-um has a minuscule body and the teeth of a Doberman pinscher. In other global places, they are called sand flies and chiggers. In Scotland, they call them midgies, or midget pests. No one is certain whether the midgies came to Charleston from Scotland or the no-see-ums headed to Scotland from Charleston. There is no doubt that they could survive the trip in either direction.

The no-see-ums are not our most famous bugs.

Everybody has heard of roaches, right? Cockroaches have survived the planet's greatest cataclysms, including the one that killed off the dinosaurs. In Charleston, they have been nurturing on old musty stuff we couldn't unload in the garage sale. Old stuff has been a beneficial delicacy to them—like giving steroids to major leaguers.

The roaches in Charleston are unlike any other. We call them palmetto bugs. They are 50 percent larger than normal roaches, and those suckers can fly. Yes, they can land on your head from a perch in a chandelier. This lifelong trauma has awakened a middle-aged Charleston woman in recurring nightmares of swatting one from her hair as a child. I know because that woman sleeps next to me and has my last name. I may have to put her in an institution.

If a Charlestonian hears that a neighbor saw a palmetto bug near a home two blocks away, the exterminator is immediately called. I know folks I grew up with who would rather face a category 5 hurricane than come face-to-face with a palmetto bug. Fear is a powerful emotion.

It is more likely that a shriek heard a half mile away is not a sewer rat, not a break-in, and not domestic violence. It is invariably a palmetto bug crawling out of a cupboard. The shrill is unmistakable. It is louder and more frazzled than an Inuit mother giving childbirth in the wilderness snow of Alaska's north slope. There is only one other varmint worse than a palmetto bug known to a Geechee.

Have you ever had a bat whisk like a fluttering wind over your sleeping noggin at night? Yes, I have. They can turn sideways and crawl through mortar cracks in a chimney. Their little beady eyes don't really see, but their radar is better than anything the Department of Defense has developed. Charleston's bat population may be exceeding the rate of growth of Charleston's cumyas. And bats are definitely benyas.

When I was eleven, I must've killed a few dozen over just one summer. I kept the broom by my bed and would react like a startled firefighter once the first bat emerged. I've killed two the same bat-evening. Every summer night was a bat-adventure in the bat-city. Their smashed carcasses could be flushed, so I sentenced them to the porcelain grave.

I hate bats. But I hate standing in lines at airports, too. I mostly hate bats at airports.

Palmetto tree silhouettes view to Charleston harbor from
Sullivans Island at sunset. Photo by author.

CHAPTER 7

Disasters Not of Our Making

WE WERE FRAUGHT with the realities of mostly our own doing. Of all the big disasters Charleston has ever encountered, the most significant cataclysm was man-made. It happened on the morning of April 12, 1861. We shouldn't have oughta done dat.

We started to do dat bee foe. It was in 1832 when we first tried to secede from the union. We even produced an Ordinance of Nullification,[16] but that silliness was quickly rendered as null. The showdown of little South Carolina versus the Feds inspired Charleston lawyer James Pettigru to comment, "South Carolina is too small for a nation and too large for an insane asylum."[17]

It can be said that our largest man-made disaster begat a series of other disasters. We were cited as one of the areas targeted for the war's aftermath—Reconstruction. The train never arrived with the lumber. Though the South would eventually be reconstructed to economic prominence, economic survival between 1860 and 1960 was on life support in the city where the war began. We did that to ourselves, as well.

After a while, we became weary of our difficult situation and needed something to take our mind off of it. The Great Charleston Earthquake of 1886 was timely. Our ancestors went to the middle of the street to get a better view of their destroyed fledgling businesses as they collapsed. The 1886 earthquake was the most massive upheaval recorded in the southeastern region of the United States—ever. Thousands of buildings were either destroyed or rendered unusable until repairs could be made. More than one hundred citizens died.[18]

The Great Charleston Earthquake was an intraplate event—very rare. That distinction didn't make it any better. How big was it? It was felt in Boston, Chicago, and Cuba. There was damage in Alabama and Ohio.[19] We forgot about the War of Northern Aggression long enough to invent earthquake rods. Check em out. They can be seen in a hundred buildings downtown. We don't know if they'll be effective because we haven't had anything like it since.

There were a few other disasters that rolled through. We won't count the fires and malaria, smallpox, and flu epidemics. The Influenza Pandemic of 1919 hit everybody. We'll stick to our own particular misfortunes.

The Holy City is a favorite target of windstorms. Imagine yourself at a dinner party. You meet Able, Cindy, Gracie, Dora, Dennis, Dottie, Kate, Hugo, Earl, Kyle, Charley, Gaston, Alberto, Hanna, Andrea, Hermine, Julia, Matthew, and Irma. Blowhards all. These are named storms that have either hit or grazed Charleston in the last seventy years. We get brushed or hit by a named storm every 2.86 years.[20]

The windstorm history is daunting, but we still come out and display our wares at the City Market as soon as the "all clear" is signaled. It's like an anthill reappears a day after it was attacked with a garden hose. Here's a rundown of the National Weather Service's historical list of direct hits since I was a toddler:

1959 (September 29) Hurricane Gracie hits with 130 miles per hour winds 40 miles to the south. Most homes lost roofs. Many windows blew in. Folly Beach unofficially reports of 140 miles per hour gusts hitting at low tide. [Personal note: A pecan tree came down and struck our home on Ashley Avenue.]

1989 (September 21) Hugo devastates area with 140 miles per hour winds & $7 billion in damage. Gusts hit 168 miles per hour at Charleston Air Force Bae. 26 were killed; five of them were children 8 years old or younger. [More on this storm is covered in a separate chapter.]

1999 (September 7). Floyd brings 80 miles per hour winds. They didn't know it was a hurricane until it left. It was coming hard but turned to Myrtle Beach.

2004 (August 14) Charley hits just east with 80 miles per hour winds.

2004 (August 29) Hurricane Gaston 75 miles per hour winds veer east. No reports of hurricane sustained winds in Charleston. Whew!

2016 (October 8) Hurricane Matthew hits with 80 miles per hour winds while moving northeast along the coast. Three deaths were reported in South Carolina. Widespread coastal flooding (6.20 feet) at Charleston.[21]

Charleston has experienced fifteen direct or direct-proximity hurricanes since 1874. Figure on a new direct hit every ten years (9.6 years by average). Some are minimal (75 miles per hour winds), while others are like 1989's Hugo (140 miles per hour winds). The real story is the timing with the tides. A storm that comes in with the high tide on the northeast quadrant brings the devastation of significant flooding. It's the force of moving water that impacts structures the most.

Hurricanes are a way of life with the Geechees. It's why so many of them have a summer home in the mountains.

A useful rule of the thumb on hurricane warnings is that you should leave if some high-placed governmental authority broadcasts instructions to "Get out!" I dishonored that rule first-hand and remembered thinking that I wasn't sure that I would outlive my poor choice (Hurricane Hugo, 1989).

Hibernian Society of Charleston Hall dates to 1841.
The famous Back Bar is where Charletonians are often over-served.
Photo by author.

CHAPTER 8

Not What You Think

THIS CITY, I suppose, is considered the Deep South. Many inferences accompany that distinction if one is not from these parts. Surely the language of Geechee-Gullah hits a melodic crescendo. Sweet tea is in every restaurant. Rice is still king. The humidity is stifling most of the year, and the breeze is the best protection we have against no-see-ums and mosquitoes.

As a "native," I have always been a bit defensive when those from afar consider us backward, uneducated, or of extreme racial bias. Those assessments are entirely unfair.

An explanation from a Geechee viewpoint may assist.

It's true we do things differently here, but never mistake cultural differences for doing something the wrong way. There are some quaint traditions and some things that could transition for the better.

The further one moves south, the slower the pace. Georgia moves slower than we do. Just ask them. In the Caribbean, they bring your silverware for breakfast if you're still at the table when lunch begins. By the time one reaches Panama, nothing happens at all. I've never seen an adult Panamanian standing up.

Others from elsewhere knock us for our faith sometimes.

It's true that we are heavy on the church attendance here (unapologetically). Outside of Mormon-centered Utah, South Carolina is among the highest percentage of church attendance states in the nation—and all of the others are southern states. It's our way. Charleston, in particular, makes Sunday a special day. Our Jewish friends are vigilant, as well, on Saturdays. Well, it is the Holy City! Those Geechees seen exiting downtown churches or synagogues will likely be dressed quite well. Attending Charleston religious services is a dressy event. Again, our traditions dictate the formality and the reverence. It really is a positive experience—given what is the norm in other parts of the world.

Some Geechees like hunting; some like fishing—and some like golf. Some like NASCAR because it brandishes tattoos on cars. You can bet the farm that they all love college football. With few exceptions, a Charlestonian is either for the Gamecocks of the University of South Carolina or for the Clemson University Tigers. Being ambivalent is not allowed. Priority stadium seating is an earned benefit and becomes a sticky issue in should a pending divorce surface. Football is Religion 102.

As far as education goes, our "K-12" schools in the Charleston area rate among the best in America. Look it up! You folks pay for it. Much of the education money comes from tourism. Other funding for higher education is derived from the state education lottery. I bet you didn't know that.

Our local colleges are also celebrated for their academic prowess. The College of Charleston is the oldest municipal college in America and charts a strong liberal arts venue. The Citadel is among the most prestigious military colleges anywhere and is consistently ranked as the #1 value in the South by U.S. News and World Report. The focus is "principled leadership in an academic environment." Charleston Southern University boasts course studies in science-based disciplines within a religious (Baptist) environment. CSU is barely fifty years old. United States Senator Tim Scott is a graduate.

We're well educated. We just don't sound like it!

As for the racial bias innuendo, I suppose there are racially biased people everywhere. It is an unwelcome side of society that has taken too much time to eviscerate. While the divides are sometimes evident here and elsewhere, local public discourse has been quite fruitful. Personally, I have never met a member of the Ku Klux Klan here or anywhere else. Happily, I have seen much of the opposite. Charleston is a place where the races, though not perfect, have made much more progress than most other locations across the country. But that area of improvement remains in a state of constant growth and understanding. We have to work at it with diligence and purpose.

Those that point fingers at our fair city should do themselves a favor. Stay a while and observe. It is likely that the perception of the Deep South characteristics embedded in the "cumya psyche" will be waylaid by the actual experience of meeting the benyas. Hope so!

When you come here, we sincerely welcome you. It is not a facade. You can do us an enormous favor by opening your mind and heart to us, as well. We hope that you'll find that our welcoming citizens are proud to be your host and hope that you will enjoy it enough to come back again. After all, we admit that we are different. We hope you'll see that difference as a positive that entices. We're Geechees, and we're proud!

Birds and clouds in panorama of Charleston Harbor
from the rooftop of People's Building.
It's the view that President William Howard Taft witnessed in 1911.
Oil on canvas by author.

CHAPTER 9

The Chamber, the CVB, and the Press

A S CHAMBERS OF Commerce go, we have an old one. It's not that the people running it are old, though they may be. It's because we have the oldest municipal Chamber of Commerce in America. It started in 1773 to thwart a British import mandate. Shortly after that, thirteen guys met in a tavern (where else?) to formally reorganize and incorporate.[22] The Chamber (now Metro Chamber of Commerce) still meets monthly and has a social mixer to follow. That old tavern gave the founders a headstart on libations in a new nation.

What started to protect the interests of plantation owners and shipping magnates now protects the interests of auto manufacturers, T-shirt factories, and digital think tanks. That diversity now defines the Lowcountry. You'll hear the term Lowcountry. It's one word, not two. It describes the flat land that runs for more than fifty miles from the beach to the sandy hills east of Columbia. It's where snakes, gators, crab, and raccoons have few places to hide. There are ample vistas of reedy growth sewn into the pluff mud. We Geechees think that pluff mud is our birthright. It should remain undisturbed and pungent.

Get used to that word Lowcountry. It's charming. The land is being described in the term. Look around. It's flat. Now, it's not as bad as Holland (called the Netherlands because it is "nether land" nor ocean). The Lowcountry is the alluvial soil that accepts the tides but allows space for walking above it—but not by much. Scientists tell us that we were under water for many years but emerged just in time to steal the waterfront views from Columbia and Charlotte. Being from the Lowcountry means that you are aware of marsh hens and coots. The older coots sometimes live in Charleston homes.

There were times when the Lowcountry business-promotion organization was called the Trident Chamber of Commerce. The trident is a mythological pitchfork with three prongs. They represented Charleston, Berkeley, and Dorchester counties. But the name was changed to Metro since the entire area benefitted with cooperation to the cause. Chambers attract established businesses, new places of commerce, and tourism—which is a business, too.

To that end, the Charleston Area Convention and Visitors Bureau (CACVB) took steroids a few years back and set new home run records. With a plan that made sense, they drew in all of the constituencies from Folly Beach to Goose Creek and beyond to build a significant networking and marketing plan. In my mind, the CACVB is among the most responsible organizations that heralded our Charleston, eventually getting the word out. Voila! We vault into travel consciousness and become a world city.

The tourist destination status—among the highest rated in the world since 2009—can be correlated to the CACVB's joint strategy of including all municipalities in their advertising campaigns. It's about all of Charleston.

The CACVB even has a sports marketing plan with noted events staged such as the Volvo Family Circle Tennis Championship and several World Golf events (1991 Ryder Cup, 1997 World Cup, 2012 PGA Championship).

With all of its growth, metro Charleston is not a major league sports city. Most residents believe that to be a blessing! As a commercial appraiser friend once told me, "Charleston has all the benefits of a large city, but none of the problems. There is very little crime, pollution, or gridlocked traffic. Yet there are ample outdoor activities to be enjoyed year-round like golf, tennis, and sailing."[23]

The Metro Chamber of Commerce has a separate sports council—The Charleston Metro Sports Commission. It is ably staffed and brings top events like college basketball tournaments and myriad other venues.

The Charleston press starts and ends with the South's oldest daily newspaper—The Post and Courier. It started as The Courier in 1803.[24] The slight name changes ensued, but the rolls of paper and barrels of ink went to the same address. I sometimes write letters-to-the-editor just to keep them straightened out and accurate, but they do not always listen. To date, they have not put a team of reporters together to investigate my "writes and wrongs," but I'll be ready! I spent some of my early life delivering their now-defunct afternoon paper, The Charleston Evening Post. I did this for income well below what child wage laws would have allowed. But I learnt!

The Evening Post Publishing Company has done well with other local area newspapers and even a book publishing company. I could send this book to them, but if they accepted it (unlikely), their process from author to Barnes and Noble Bookstores could outlast me. However, they have a class organization even without my favorite unembellished local author within their inventory.

Other publications exist. I wrote for a few. I once was the sports editor of my college newspaper at The Citadel, The Brigadier. It survived after my 1974 graduation. I wrote over one hundred columns for The Lowcountry Sun. It went out of publication in 2015. I had nothing to do with that outcome, I swear!

Charleston has a kaleidoscope of lovely magazines including Charleston Weddings. The devotion to this tradition has vaulted Charleston to the top setting in America for destination weddings. There's no doubt that weddings will take two people for a ride!

I have not subscribed to several top magazine publications because the actual articles are usually about one-third of the content. That does not mean that the magazines are not spectacular. They are. I see them in waiting rooms, at my doctor's office, in the barbershop, and at most places where we were trained to hurry up and wait. I should not brag about my cheap self, but truth becomes me. The ones that have really impressed me are Charleston Magazine, Charleston Living Magazine, Mount Pleasant Magazine, and Playboy. I just threw that last one in there to keep you awake. I never see that one in the barbershop.

I did want to cite The Charleston Mercury because my favorite college professor, James Rembert, has written articles in it for many years. His Citadel English Department course on satire compelled me to a lifetime of not taking anything too seriously except what satirists wrote. The good professor has a high tolerance for Geechee. He is one.

Combined, Charleston's commercial marketing and its press have been around longer than any other city in America. And we're just hitting our stride.

Marketing Charleston used to be a challenge. It just ain't that way no mo.

Chevaux de Frise.
Example of the physical measure taken by some Charlestonians in the early 1800s to dissuade home invasions. Photo by author.

CHAPTER 10

What Was and Wasn't

CHARLESTONIANS ARE OFTEN asked, "What was it like here before?" There seems to be a fascination of the phoenix-like rise of the Holy City. Of course, we're talking about the mythological phoenix, not that sprawling city without water in Arizona. The apt description of the mythology fits. The legendary bird dies in a fire of its own making and then rises from its own ashes. Yeah, that's Charleston!

The question of what we were like, I assume, portends to the decades before the Spoleto Festival found us (1977). Benyas have been calling the creatures that come to Charleston for this one-of-a-kind art extravaganza the "Spoletians." It is as if they arrive from another planet in a distant galaxy. Yet it is a term of endearment. Why? Spoleto Festival USA is the catalyst event that changed the Holy City's trajectory. But before Spoleto, what was this backwater peninsula of latent doom?

We can travel back a few years further to make the contrast stark.

A modern visitor might ask what did we had; and what was missing? Got it. Let's ruminate!

Way back when we had artesian wells of free water that flowed for anyone to collect at two well points across the city. People stopped and filled heavy glass gallon jugs. The water was clear and healthy. It came from wells dug in 1881 down nearly 1,700 feet.[25] The wells were not shut down until more than one hundred years later (1989) because of Hurricane Hugo.[26] As a youngster, one of the wells was only a block from us on Calhoun Street. I never understood why the water ran continuously. Mark that down on the list of the other four million things I don't understand.

We had old buses on old bus routes, but they were never even half-full. You could get on one with a wooden token or a dime. Those buses could not have made a profit. It was either that, or the passengers departed before the buses arrived near our corner. I suppose we could have taken the city bus to school on rainy days. We never did. A dime was too much money.

We had a few chain stores in Charleston like Woolworths, W.T. Grants, and Sears—all on King Street. Even so, much of the local shopping went to local merchants like Kerrisons, Croghans, Condons, Krawchecks, Dixie Furniture, and Berlins. Only Croghans and Berlins remain (both over a century in business). We bought local then and still do! Personally, I think locally owned is what edifies King Street as one of the great mercantile streets in America today.

We have things laying around in Charleston that don't fit anything. For instance, we never removed the large carriage stones near the curbs. Notice these as you walk the city. It was where ladies, especially, dismounted from the old horse carriages. They make great conversation subjects. It's because 99 percent of visitors have no idea what they are and why they are still in place.

Our old gas-lit street lamps are not old. Those all rusted out or blew away in any number of hurricanes. The reproduction lamps are gas-lit. They'll be here for a few more hurricanes.

You may hear French words spoken by the real Geechee tour guides. They'll say Shay-Vo-de-Free. That's Geechee French for "Chevaux de Frise." These are spikes on spindles that were put up to dissuade a home invasion in the immediate aftermath of the Denmark Vesey failed slave revolt of 1822.[27] The French language purists insist it means curly or spiked hair. They're wrong. I'm right. Chevaux de Frise is a reference to the Frisian Horses used in cavalry charges during a Spanish war with Holland.[28] Wooden spikes were placed into logs to stop the Frisian horses. There you have it. Do not go into a fine Charleston restaurant and order Chevaux de Frise for two.

The cobblestones pre-date America. They are still the predominant roadbeds at Chalmers Street and North Adgers Wharf. In old Charleston lore, a husband was to take his pregnant wife down one of these bumpy roads if she was well past her due date for childbirth. They were called "Labor Lanes." I never believed that one because there would have to be a willing wife involved. The cobblestones are not native to the area. They were weight ballasts for sailing ships. In all, seven streets still have a cobblestone roadbed within the peninsula. Cobblestone roads once totaled ten miles of paved passageway on the peninsula. The cobblestones are still under just about every major street.

What cultural items we identify from way back when include Royal Crown Cola, Burger Beer, and AM station 1250 on the radio. Telephones came here after the rest of the world had them for years. They still weren't speaking to us. We had five-digit phone numbers. My grandmother's number was 2-7938. Ours was 2-3657. And there were party lines. Sometimes there would be a conversation on the phone line from someplace else. It was its own form of new entertainment.

There were essentially three pods of industry and commerce in the Holy City. Tourism was not one of them. Workers were needed at the State Ports, the Charleston Naval Shipyard, or the hospital complex. There wasn't much else. Accordingly, there were few fortunes made in Charleston. Lacking growth, the real estate market was a long and struggling "flat-liner." Jolts to the employment index were rare.

When television came to Charleston in 1953 (WCSC went live)[29] we didn't know if the on-camera personnel were in New York, Hollywood, or Charleston. With only three eventual stations, we figured it out. Local celebrities were created. Everything went off at midnight except a still rendering of a Native American in a circle and a low sound tone. My dad slept most nights to the "buzz of the Chief." Now we have a remote and leave on something soothing like World War II in Color or The Walking Dead. In the 1950s and into the 1960s, there was only one black and white television in a home and plenty of spare tubes when it broke. The attraction to a movie theater was that everything was more realistic because they had Technicolor. I suppose that Charleston was not too much different than Wichita or Poughkeepsie.

The movie houses and the drive-in theaters were our extravagances. There were four theaters along King Street—the American, the Gloria, the Garden, and the Riviera. The Drive-Ins that I remember were the North 52 and the Magnolia. The sound from those metal post speakers was awful. But I'm told that some attendees never watched the movies anyway.

Even back then, it has been said that we Geechees were mannerly citizens. This is not to say that other places did not have manners. It seems that the difficult decades we knew here exuded in manners from everyone—all economic levels, races, and creeds. Charleston's attention to friendliness, helpfulness, and admirable manners defined us for many

Rainbow Row was just a group of drab buildings dating back to 1740 until they were painted in pastel colors in the 1930s. Photo by author.

years beyond. It has much to do with why visitors never hear car horns. Only an excitable passer-through would dare blow a horn in our quiet paradise! Invariably, it's a retired cabbie from New York City. At least, that's what I tell folks if I hear one.

By the late 1950's the characters that pushed carts and delivered block ice began to fade away. Surely the ice began to melt. We saw the vegetable and crab carts (or rather heard them) coming. They had it all. Fresh food included snap beans, cob corn, cabbage, watermelon, and "maters." The tomatoes came from Johns Island, much like the rest of the cart inventory. When the cargo ships docked from Cuba, we had bananas and sugar cane. The crab and fresh shrimp were caught locally and iced down. The street cart vendors were known for their piercing vocals upon approach. They did not need megaphones. One might hear, "Snap beans, fresh fush, shugah cane, cahn—sweet cahn!" It was a song of beauty. They always sold out.

The block ice trucks delivered to the old iceboxes on a schedule— well after the introduction of residential refrigeration. Geechee Charlestonians couldn't just go out and buy a new refrigerator when tradition told them that an icebox worked just fine. Besides, there wasn't a lot of money—even in our small banks.

My farm-raised grandfather still mowed the grass with a spindle bladed hand push mower. There was no gas to fool with, and no bag for the clippings. Of course, it helped that my grandpa was also among the most frugal people whom I ever knew. The finely coiffured grass had a natural and relentless adversary—us! We wore it out in several baseball-obvious places. He didn't seem to mind. It was less grass to cut. My grandfather did not have the only spindle bladed grass mower in Charleston. They were quite common.

People ate every meal, every day, at home on a table with no television. Most families returned thanks. We had to pray that my mother got the pork chops out of the oven before the fire marshal arrived.

In a family with nine children, meals were an accounting. If you weren't there, you didn't eat. It was my dad's rule. Even though my mother was an awful cook, we still placed her on a pedestal. We had to do that to keep my dad away!

There were no fast food establishments and scant formal restaurants. The 1950s and 1960s boasted of Henry's, Perdita's, the Cavallaro (West Ashley with dancing and brown bag liquor), and La Brasca's Italian.

There were no Tex-Mex or Chinese food eateries within a hundred miles or more. Though La Brasca's had pizza, there was no delivery. Ah, pizza. I'm salivating right now! The first day that my dad brought a take-out pizza home from La Brasca's I shied away from eating it because I didn't know what it was. Meanwhile, those other siblings went into a feeding frenzy. I couldn't even get a sniff of the cardboard box.

Charleston had its share of perils back then, as now. The treacherous sidewalks remain. They are our gift of adventure to tourists and emergency room doctors. Live oak roots can break concrete, separate cobblestones, and bricks, and lift thick slate. The result is that a casual walker has to look down or they will end up down looking up.

Like elsewhere, we had police cars with red lights, not blue. We had cigarettes with no warning labels. But the surgeon general's 1964 report killed off our Rainbow Row ashtray industry.

The community had a baby elephant, Suzie Q, grazing at a local television tower, and a three-legged lion at the Hampton Park Zoo. Yes, we had a zoo. But nobody went there because we had mostly snakes and alligators. And it reeked of odors that could water your eyes! Once the zoo mercifully closed down, Hampton Park Zoo became Hampton Park. It's still Hampton Park. The odd and exotic animals moved to the next adjacent site—The Citadel. With hard work, those animals can graduate in four years.

Traditions marked time. Most Charleston families knew to replace the family heirloom Persian rug in the parlor with the braided or Jute summer rug. It was the law. It was much like what my brother Danny told his Citadel freshman roommate from Pennsylvania: "We have to climb the live oaks to take down the summer moss and put up the winter moss each year." Though that was a ruse, the rug exchange season was real. My grandmother changed out her rugs each season. It was as if the hardwood flooring put up its sweater and pulled out a tee shirt.

There were things the city did not have and still doesn't have. There were few wide streets and too many thin alleyways. The sewer pipes were on loan from ancient Pompeii. There was no stormwater drainage plan. Today, we blame the melting Arctic Ice Cap on our newer stormwater problems. Hard rains or full moon tides flood Charleston streets. When we have a summer solstice, a high tide, a full moon, and a monsoon-like rainstorm, the Uber drivers opt for gondolas. We even have sun floods.

That's a term used to signify flooding on the usual streets when there is no rain whatsoever.

We now have a stormwater plan that has mitigated some flooding. We have nothing to mitigate the full moon tides and occasional windstorms.

It is laughable that the serious cyclists are petitioning to get bike lanes all across the peninsula. I like biking as well as anyone. But there are places in the Holy City where two cars cannot pass. Many streets have pullover places to allow for oncoming traffic. The city was built for pedestrians and horses. The retrofit to cars has been difficult enough. The solution is easy. Dig fifty-five feet down to reach the clay-like marl. Install bike lanes. There. Done.

You've read that there were very few tourists years ago because there were no hotels with air conditioning. There were few homes with air conditioning. Or offices. One could walk into a downtown bank and stay in line under the wide ceiling fans on purpose with no banking plans. No deposit necessary. In the old Charleston homes, an oscillating fan provided a harsh noise that was overlooked because of the movement of a breeze. It was heaven.

On the bright side, we had very little crime in my youthful Charleston—unless you count stolen bicycles. It was sad that my parents wouldn't let us just go steal one back. Dad-gummed ethics! We had no street gangs or thugs, very little traffic congestion, and almost no vehicular pollution. Everybody knew everybody. It was just that cozy. People left their front doors unlocked and their screened windows open. The unscreened windows invited critters from squirrels to palmetto bugs. You already know that palmetto bugs are Charleston roaches with high IQs and devious intentions. Ask any fine Charleston lady.

As a family, we had experiences and foibles that others had. We had pets. We didn't buy them. We once had stray kittens, but brother David placed them in a mailbox for safekeeping. They were still there when he got back from school, but not moving quite as well. For those horrified in the PETA ranks, I have David's address and phone number.

We had fig trees and a few figs that the June bugs didn't devour. Some of them got an early start in late May. We had the jujube tree, too, along with six pecan trees. My dad brought home industrial brown bags from a trucking company that we used to fill up with pecans. We sold them for twenty-five cents to people leaving the hospital. We sold out every time. Pity is a powerful sales tool.

We had a four-line clothesline. My grandmother needed it to dry the sheets in the guest rooms. Why I mention it is because she had a pail of old-style wooden clothespins. There were no metal springs on the old hanging pins. I'm told that when I was a toddler, my mother used one of the wooden pins on my one curly ear to try and straighten it. She wanted to take me places without people asking, "What's wrong with his ear?" The plan didn't work. I have a naturally curly ear that still hears well, despite my mother's attempts to make me appear normal.

For sheer fun, my granny had a joggling board painted Charleston green (black) that stayed in the shade under her front piazza. Mentally, I can place myself there now. I'm glad that board joggled my memory about other crazy stuff in that yard. There was a turtle pond. It was built around 1900 by my great-grandfather to raise diamondback terrapins. It was thought that diamondback terrapin soup eased the pain of arthritis. They also had a small goldfish pond with water lilies. The National Convention of Bull Frogs met at that pond every August.

There were deer antlers galore all over the family home. Some ancestor hunted and wanted to remember each of his prey fawnly. I never had venison as a child. I have to wonder where all that deer meat went? Come to think of it, my frugal grandfather was likely raised on venison.

My mother's mother's father had a bird egg collection—with enough eggs to fill a museum. That's where they went—to the Charleston Museum. But I still have a 100-year-old ostrich egg. Anybody? It should hatch any day now.

What was not there? There were no golf clubs, no billiard table, and no croquet. There was no leftover saddles or swords from the "recent unpleasantness," nor a musket from the Revolution. There was a sword, but it was a dress sword from the Knights of Columbus. It showed no bloodstains from killing heathens. We never saw a snow shovel or a hockey stick. There was no suntan lotion in the cabinet, just old horsehair shaving brushes. Those were for the women. The men used a bowie knife.

My granny had an old-fashioned manual typewriter. She likely found it abandoned at an archeological dig. I placed the manufacture year between the George Washington and James Monroe administrations.

She typed on it accurately with poor eyesight and no training. She was a chemistry major (College of Charleston 1923). Yet she fought that old typewriter to write historical articles, several small publications, and a full-blown book. She had to have incredible patience with herself.

Our home had no coat closet. We think it was because we had no coats. There were no musical instruments, and we had no stereo system. We had to limit our prowess in that area of culture to the jingles the nuns taught us at school.

We never got dessert. Never. But we did chase down the Popsicle wagon one time when it made a wrong turn down Ashley Avenue. That fool never came back.

We had a lot of Band-Aids. With nine children, we seemed to run a tin box out each week. We had toothpaste tubes that were contorted and hammered to get every morsel out. My mother put methylate on every cut, bite, and blister. It left an orangish-red stain. We were right ugly even before those colorful applications of methylate.

My granny had two items of antiquity on her lower brick porch—millstones once used to grind grain for flower, and an iron-iron. The iron-iron was black and made of iron. It was heavy. Years ago, this iron was placed on a stove to absorb heat and iron clothing. We don't know what happened to that iron-iron. It's gone-gone.

We didn't have a supermarket, a shopping center, or an ice skating rink.

We didn't have coyotes. We have them now.

We had a city dump, but it was wherever the city needed to slow down the tidal encroachment. No one had ever heard of an environmental hazard. I know of many "late model" Charleston homes built over what was the city dump of my youth.

We didn't have an asylum. All of our crazy people were sent to Columbia. No, wait. That's still ongoing. But now we call them representatives to the state legislature.

In summary, Charleston had a lot for not having had much, and the McQueeneys had more than many others, but still had very little.

BENYAS AND CUMYAS

Charleston's Powder Magazine is the oldest
public building in the city (1713).
Captured by the British during the American Revolution.
Photo by author.

CHAPTER 11

The Swamp Fox

AS A YOUNG and impressionable Geechee, I enjoyed the Walt Disney episodes that we gathered to see on Sunday evenings. It was a rotating miniseries that extolled the previously unheralded patriotism of Colonel Francis Marion. It was shot in Hollywood in 1959. I was seven.

The precryogenic Walt Disney introduced the first episode by saying, "Outside of George Washington, Francis Marion was the largest hero of the American Revolution." I'm down with that.

The role of Colonel Francis Marion, the Swamp Fox, was played by a man we later embraced as a comedic actor, Leslie Nielsen (Naked Gun series). The clever colonel found ways to delay or divert the British Army in South Carolina. He was adept at guerilla warfare. His attacks on supply lines to British general Cornwallis's army changed the dynamic of the Revolution in the South. That's historical fact.

Once Charleston fell, the British had a major port. But they could not capitalize and establish supremacy. The Swamp Fox changed their plans. By the time they made their way up near the North Carolina line at Cowpens, they were run from the field of battle—a startling turnaround.

Though militarily superior, they continued to blunder at the hands of the guerrilla fighters. The tactics were essential, and the British plan to chase General Greene led to another Cornwallis blunder that ended the war. He ran into George Washington's forces at the Yorktown peninsula without adequate supplies. His retreat was blocked by General LaFayette and the French naval forces in the Chesapeake Bay. Cornwallis surrendered. His defeated troops did not sing the Disney jingle:

Swamp Fox, Swamp Fox, tail on his hat
Nobody knows where the Swamp Fox is at.

Never end a sentence a preposition with. I'm betting the song was contrived by the Mickey Mouse Singers. It was actually sung by Leslie Nielsen![30] In any event, Francis Marion had a whole forest named for him, and then a county, and a town, and a college, and the main square in Charleston. The tall colonnade statue that overlooks Marion Square is not Francis Marion. It's John C. Calhoun, the U.S. vice president under both John Quincy Adams and Andrew Jackson. Andrew Jackson was born in South Carolina, as well. Imagine—we were the home state of the sitting president and the sitting vice president. Big deal, right? Nope. They didn't get along.

The loose use of Mel Gibson as the same characterization (based on Francis Marion) in the blockbuster movie, The Patriot, was filmed in Charleston. They put dirt on our streets then swept it all back up. Mel was here. But the movie script took many liberties to entertain. Time Magazine ranked it as one of the top ten historically inaccurate stories of all time.[31] Let's see if Time bothers to rate this book.

Francis Marion died in 1795 at the age of sixty-three and is buried at Belle Isle Plantation (Berkeley County). As of this writing, Mel Gibson is only sixty-two. He and Leslie Nielsen look nothing alike. And the real Revolutionary War hero, Francis Marion, looked nothing like either of them.

Francis Marion's guerrilla tactics are part of the military training of the Army's Green Beret. His ability to disrupt supplies and communications in the face of overwhelming odds had distinguished his career.

Charleston has an elegant old hotel (built in 1924) that became one of our early skyscrapers at twelve stories. In Charleston, a structure reaching skyward for twelve floors will qualify it as a monstrosity. The Francis Marion Hotel has 235 guest rooms and was the largest hotel in the Carolinas when it was completed—in those humid days without air conditioning.[32] With brilliant renovations, it still stands as a Charleston landmark. The often-renovated Francis Marion Hotel pays homage to a Lowcountry hero who changed the course of United States history.

The General P.G.T. Beauregard quarters at 192 Ashley
Avenue during the firing on Fort Sumter.
Photo by author.

CHAPTER 12

Give My Regard to Beauregard

PIERRE GUSTAVE TOUTANT Beauregard was not from these parts. He was a West Point graduate from Louisiana who distinguished himself in the Mexican War (1846).[33] He was a small but dashing man who was appointed as superintendent at West Point before resigning his post to command the defense of Charleston in 1860. Apparently, there were those of great military pedigree who assumed that a war was imminent.

His friends never called him Pierre, or Gussy, or Toutant. He used his initials "GT" and accepted the nickname Bory. He dropped Pierre, but historians tacked it back on. His actual expertise was as a military engineer.[34]

General Beauregard gave the order to start the Civil War. It was because, according to him, Union commander Major Robert Anderson (who was born in Louisville, Kentucky) just wouldn't leave well enough alone. Things went south before Major Anderson surrendered and went north. You would think that two grown men would have come up with a better solution than to start a war.

Had times been different, his name would have emerged as an excellent leader of men. He was well respected within the U.S. Army prior to his defection to the Confederacy on the grounds of his native Louisiana birth.

The Union and the CSA placed differing names on the battles of the same place. It was meant to confuse historians. Case in point—Bory Beauregard led his troops to a convincing win at the First Battle of Bull Run. From the Confederate point of view, they called that First Manassas. The ghosts of both sides still can't agree on the battle names.

He did much more.

Beauregard commanded armies in the Western Theater, including the Battle of Shiloh in Tennessee, and the Siege of Corinth in Northern

Mississippi. He returned to Charleston and defended it from repeated naval and land attacks in 1863. Arguably, his greatest achievement was saving the city of Petersburg, Virginia, and thus also the Confederate capital of Richmond, from assaults by overwhelmingly superior Union Army forces in the June of 1864. However, his influence over Confederate strategy was marred by his poor relationships with Confederate President Jefferson Davis and other generals. In April 1865, Beauregard and his commander, General Joseph E. Johnston, convinced Davis and the remaining cabinet members that the war needed to end, and the majority of the remaining Confederate armies were surrendered to Sherman.[35]

So, the man that started the war was consequential in ending the war. Good on him. This history lesson is rendered to you because the man with the fine French name spent time in Charleston and wooed the local ladies with his charm. They saw him as women may have swooned over Tom Cruise, Richard Gere, or Bradley Cooper. He once lived at 192 Ashley Avenue. The 192 Ashley Avenue home is a mansion that is just down a bit from the animal enclosure where I was raised at 141 Ashley Avenue. That residence put him out of range from the Union cannon fire that bombarded Charleston for 567 days. That bombardment remains as the most protracted siege of a city in world history. Charleston fell just weeks before Lee's surrender at Appomattox Court House, Virginia.

The swooning ladies in Charleston during Beauregard's first duty here had no movies or television to divert them, so they used that time to chase the general. They threw themselves at the French-Cajun. He was a snazzy dresser with impeccable manners. He received hundreds of letters and assorted personal gifts from scarves to flowers and pins. The fact that he had a wife and three children back in New Orleans didn't seem to dissuade the Charleston femmes. But his popularity in the suffering south after the war diminished. Why? It was because he was among the first to embrace racial equality, a hundred years before the Civil Rights Act.

'I am persuaded' that the natural relation between the white and colored people is that of friendship," Beauregard said in an address published in July 1873 in newspapers including The New Orleans Republican and The Daily Picayune. "I am persuaded that their interests are identical; that their destinies in this state, where the two races are equally divided, are linked together; and that there is no prosperity for Louisiana which must not be the result of their cooperation.[36]

A statue of "no-more-Pierre" Gustave Toutant Beauregard stands in New Orleans. A memorial arch of Beauregard is in Washington Square Park in Charleston. It's on the back wall. Ladies, it's traditional to leave a scarf.

We Geechees give homage to the historical characters that have had the "Real Charleston" experience. General Beauregard made the list because he was honest, effective, and convincing. His post-war views were spot on, even if unpopular in his era. I once had a friend who had two bulldogs. One was "Beau Regard," the other "No Regard."

The Dock Street Theater.
Photo by author.

CHAPTER 13

Spooky

DON'T LOOK NOW, but the eyes are on you. There is a Charleston ghost just over your left shoulder. She's been following you since you picked up this book. I know the ghost is a she by the alluring shape of the apparition. You should know that I have assigned a different Charleston ghost to every book sold. You got lucky. Some of the ghosts I've contracted are dastardly representations of their former selves.

Lemme splain.

Of all the categories of interest that a destination might enjoy—best beaches, the best place to play tennis, best wedding setting, etc., the one that should appeal to the fewest would be best place to see ghosts. Savannah is better for the spirits and the apparitions. They have rows of bars on River Street that can concoct the most apparitions in America. All of our ghosts' cousins live in Savannah. Nonetheless, there are haunts-a-plenty here.

The Ghost of Room 10, at a local bed-and-breakfast, would wait until the lady occupant retires to bed before he would begin stroking her hair.[37] It's been reported enough that patrons only rent that room as a challenge bet. It makes for a hairy night. Not to be outdone, Room 8 has a less frequent visitor in the same bed-and-breakfast (hint: it's on the Battery). It's a returning soldier of the Confederate Army.[38] We have no idea what he looks like because he lost his head in battle. The headless ghost seems a bit disoriented, but his GPS keeps routing him to the right place. Don't be startled. He is harmless and has never spoken to anyone since his first appearance over a hundred years ago.

You'll find the ghost of Lavinia Fisher at the Old Jail. Lavinia and her husband John were thought to be Charleston's first serial killers more than two hundred years ago. They were caught, convicted, and hanged at the jail. But they just couldn't leave well enough alone. John and Lavinia Fisher still roam the Old Jail at night.[39] Locals can hear them wailing. The shouts are not about their innocence, but about the jailer who pulled the trap door—the very same mechanism they used to dispose of their poisoned victims. Their trap door went from their rented hotel bed to a pit. Too many victims fell for it. But the jailer's trap door swung down once the executioner placed the nooses. Justice was served, but this justice remains loud enough often enough in the wee hours of the morning.

Are you spooked yet? This city has been around long enough to have a ghosts' convention. They could all appear over a harrowing weekend.

A few years ago, I visited an employee and her husband who were renting the very same house that the Gentleman Pirate Stede Bonnet had occupied 300 years ago. The employee had just delivered their first child.

Stede Bonnet was born into wealth and got married to a lady named Mary Alamby in Barbados. All was well except for her nagging. According to records, Bonnet was driven to "pyracy" by Mary's incessant griping and the "[d]iscomforts he found in a married State."[40] He left Mary and his four children to do something else that did not require him to confront her each day. Pirate Stede performed some terrible acts, including the practice of keel-hauling hostages for ransom. Argh! Charlestonians had enough of Stede the Pirate, though he may have been a gentleman. Colonel William Rhett chased him down to the Outer Banks of North Carolina and brought him and his twenty-nine men back to be hanged in 1718. They met their end at White Point Gardens. There is a monument near the spot. Though other pirates like Richard Worley were hung there, the gentleman Bonnet is the only one with a dedicated monument. It may have been a better ending than what a nagging wife in Barbados may have entailed.

Once I recounted what I knew of the Stede Bonnet piracy story to the employee and her husband, they told me about odd noises they often heard in the upstairs room. The noises began when they moved in. Within months, the young couple and their newborn baby moved to Ohio. I hope she reads this part of the book. Ghosts aren't the only ones to make funny noises at night. Sometimes newborn babies do that.

Just to set the record straight, many old-time Charlestonians outside of the tourist industry relate with certainty that the Stede Bonnet residence is indeed haunted. It may be. Its next-door neighbor is the graveyard at St. Philips Church.

Piracy was a big deal in pre-Revolutionary Charleston. Blackbeard, or Edward Teach, liked the new deepwater port. The city was barely fifty years old when the pirate first arrived in 1718. He captured the city for a few days while trying to find medicine for his venereal disease. His ghostly figure did not stay. He, too, was captured at North Carolina's Outer Banks. Pirates should have known to avoid this area. Blackbeard's ghost has appeared in other locales as headless. So how would we know whether he's still looking for medicine here or not? How would we know that it's him? It could be any number of headless ghosts.

Some Geechee ghosts are rather quiet. They would be more popular in the silent film industry. To wit, that graveyard mentioned above at St. Philips Church dates back to 1768. But the current church was rebuilt after a fire in 1838. It's likely the most photographed church in Charleston since it juts out into the middle of the street. Print and digital photographers have recorded photos of a female apparition bent over a grave there. As the story goes, a woman gave birth to a stillborn child who was buried there many years ago.[41] The mother died of the blood loss hours later. They are buried next to each other. The apparition appears more evident in the diminishing sunlight, near the reported time of the birth—as the evening arrived. I always leave graveyards before the sun goes down. It's a good rule. I declare. I ain't scade a nuttin.

There have been reports of a Union Soldier smelling of gunpowder roaming Fort Sumter. Tourists swear by the apparition. But no Union Soldier was killed in the battle of Fort Sumter (April 12-13, 1861). That's an amazing fact after that heavy thirty-four-hour bombardment. So, who could this apparition be? My guess is a fireworks expert (gunpowder smell) who works for the Charleston RiverDogs minor league baseball team. After all, the apparition has never been reported during the off-season.

I have a friend who owned an Italian restaurant (again on Church Street, the most haunted street in the city). They had to quit locking the interior doors at Bocci's because the doors would mysteriously be forced open, found inexplicably unlocked, or be banged on in the middle of the night. One of the restaurant workers saw a figure in the closed-door upstairs bathroom mirror that was not hers. She reported the incident to the owner, but no one left the restaurant with an unpaid check. It was the claustrophobic Ghost of Garlic Toast, no doubt.

The Dock Street Theatre site dates from 1736. Yes, that's on Church Street, too. It was once converted to a hotel prior to the Civil Swivel. With multiple renovations, what you see today is a very old theater with period antiques from all over Charleston that may resemble the 1736 version of the former Dock Street Theater. Nonetheless, it is stunning. But a fire destroyed much of the building in December of 1860. The celebrity Bobby Lee was in town that night (General Robert E. Lee). There were some casualties of the fire. We only know this because of strange and unintelligible voices coming from the theater sporadically. The normal and intelligible voices come from the Footlight Players on a performance schedule.

The USS Yorktown aircraft carrier overlooks Charleston Harbor. It is perhaps the most enthralling military museum and activities center in America. The nicknamed "Fighting Lady" also has a ghost. No, really. Witnesses have seen a large moving dark glob move throughout. Since they have security cameras they also have a ghost on film. Go there and ask. You decide.

Perhaps the most significant spooky storyteller ever known once lived in Charleston. Edgar Allan Poe (The Cask of Amontillado, The Tell-Tale Heart) was stationed at Fort Moultrie just a few years after our second war of independence—the War of 1812. The referee botched a few calls and that war ended up in a tie.

Poe created characters, but as far as we know, he didn't leave any behind. Though he spent much of his duty time on Sullivans Island where he arrived in the Army at age eighteen, he liked to have a drink or two at the King Charles Inn property on Meeting Street.[42] It is believed that the inspiration for his last poem, Annabel Lee, was from a sea tale he heard in Charleston. He wrote The Gold Bug fifteen years after he left Charleston. Gold Bug Island existed then as it does now on the way to Fort Moultrie. Poe died in 1847. There is no doubt that Poe was a genius with the pen.

Come to think of it, it could have been "The Raven" tapping at Bocci's door.

This is just a stab in the dark, but Charleston has never hosted Jack the Ripper or Count Dracula. So, it's hard to sink our teeth into these persistent ghoulish stories—especially when the real Charleston stories are even better.

The palmetto is the state tree. Note the quarter moon.
It has been coming around for a while.
Photo by author.

CHAPTER 14

Abner Doubleday Slid Home

W E NEVER SEE scribbling on the wall that says, "Abner was here!" He was. Abner Doubleday was credited, but not quite certified, as the inventor of our national pastime—baseball. He spent time here, too. You'll never guess where.

In recounting a man's life—who did not have the advantage of airlines, computers, or high-speed rail—Abner Doubleday stands out. The general perception is that Lil Abner put together rules for baseball in 1839 at a pasture near Cooperstown, New York. Now you understand why the Baseball Hall of Fame is in Cooperstown. Doubleday Field stands there today. He was from nearby Auburn, New York. The story was handed down, but not necessarily written down. It could be true. Who's to say? Trouble is, Abner Doubleday never bragged about inventing baseball, and the invention of baseball was not mentioned in his obituary. Then again, there may not have been room for his minor accolades. This man was a giant of accomplishment.

He had quite a pedigree. His paternal grandfather fought in the American Revolution. His maternal grandfather was a fourteen-year-old personal messenger for George Washington during the American Revolution.[43] It gets even better. His maternal great-grandfather was a Minuteman, and his father fought in the War of 1812 and became a member of the U.S. House of Representatives from Auburn, New York. Abner went to Cooperstown before it was that Cooperstown for preparatory school. It was before he entered West Point.[44]

Captain Abner Doubleday was second-in-command in the defense of Fort Sumter in Charleston Harbor. On April 12, 1861, he fired the first Union shot of the Civil War. He remained proud of that distinction over his lifetime. That fact made it into his obituary.

Doubleday, nicknamed Forty-Eight Hours by his Union soldiers, had an impressive military career. After graduating from West Point, he fought in the Mexican War (1846-48). Doubleday participated in the Seminole War of 1856. He distinguished himself in other crucial Civil War battles, rising to the rank of brigadier general. He was in a command at Gettysburg and was instrumental in saving many Union lives by defending a strategic retreat at Little Round Top. His Forrest-Gump-like battle presence reads Second Bull Run, Antietam, South Mountain, Chancellorsville, and Fredericksburg in addition to Gettysburg. He was thrown from his horse by cannon fire and wounded in the neck in separate actions. His gallantry was unquestioned.

When Abraham Lincoln was on a train to Gettysburg and scribbling a note for an address, the accompanying soldier sitting with him was our friend Abner Doubleday. He was everywhere. He may have even suggested "Four score and seven years ago" instead of "Eighty-seven years ago." Who knows?

After the war, Abner went to San Francisco where he took out a patent for a cable car railway that still runs in the City by the Bay. Yes, it's the same guy on the left coast. He moved to New Jersey after his military retirement and became the president of the Theosophy Society. He was succeeded as the society's president by Thomas Edison.[45] You just can't make this stuff up!

Though baseball historians have generally debunked Doubleday's designation as the inventor of baseball, they have not debunked that it could have happened. Doubleday did provide bats and balls to his troops during the Civil War to play the game under New York rules. He wrote out the New York rules. That part is notated. Methinks that the guy was so busy and died so suddenly (heart attack) that he may not have had time to write it all down.

If you get half a chance, take a double look at the doubly incredible life of Abner Doubleday. Geechees are respectful when a Yankee lives a productive life. We heard that it can happen in other places outside of Charleston!

The trade route by water was improved by Wappoo
Cut in pre-Revolutionary times.
Photo by author.

CHAPTER 15

Tuscarora Jack Barnwell

BEFORE THERE WAS pop culture; before there was Zorro, Indiana Jones, and Tarzan, there was Tuscarora Jack. He was likely the greatest real adventurist of our years under British rule.

A Dubliner, born John Barnwell, Tuscarora Jack came to Charles Towne when he was thirty to respond to an offer to map and survey interior lands. Trade routes needed to be established. He saw an opportunity to open trade with the many friendly tribes.

When a Scottish party settled near the Tuscarora Indians in North Carolina, a conflict was in order. The Tuscarora had six settlements in the same area and one thousand fighting men. They were forcing the Scots out in vigor. Barnwell knew much about the native culture by virtue of his relationships with other tribes. He was summoned to resolve the conflict.

The adventurer took thirty white men and 250 local Indians from various tribes. His strategic movements outmaneuvered the superior force of the Tuscarora. He dealt with them by the division of their settlements. In a few months, he had won significant victories and had pinned down the remaining Tuscarora. In response, the Tuscarora had taken several white hostages. Because of the hostages, a treaty settled the conflict. And our adventurous Jack landed a catchy nickname.

Barnwell made the region safe for trade. The descendants of Tuscarora Jack Barnwell still live here in Charleston more than three hundred years later. So, they were safe, as well. The names that filtered down to Charleston Society from Barnwell's marriage (to wife, Anne) and eight issues include the later lineage to some prominent Charleston names—Gibbes, Grimball, Sams, and too many Barnwells to count. Counties and towns in three states are named for the legendary Tuscarora Jack.

Our adventurer continued to make strides (literally) toward permanent trading routes. He established a significant fortification at Darien, Georgia, to protect the established trade route. If going, check out the discount outlet shops.

Barnwell also founded the town of Beaufort, South Carolina. They are our Geechee-Gullah cousins. He did well there! Beaufort is gorgeous. In fact, it is a "beau"tiful fort town. It was so pleasant that Parris Island Marine Corps Training Center became another handsome military base just across the river. Semper fi!

Barnwell fortified Port Royal with another fort, which protected lands that he owned—nearly 6,500 acres. Being a talented mapmaker, he charted much of the Lowcountry and beyond. His commercial interest was in the rice business and fur trading with the British.

He suggested positions of other forts along the perimeter of Georgia to dissuade encroachment by the Spanish. The man had a plan.

His former allies, the Yemassee Indians, made a policy reversal without sending a delegation seeking diplomacy. They rose up with intentions to force the settlement of Charles Towne to close up shop. Tuscarora Jack received word of the pending confrontation. His maneuvers proved brilliant and the defeated the Yemassees (along with their allies of Choctaw, Creek, and Catawbas). The tribes were forced south to Florida. Tuscarora Jack saved the colonists yet again.

This episode, "The Yemassee Indian War," had calamitous results for the original owners of the Carolinas—the eight Lord's Proprietors. They could not defend their investment. Tuscarora Jack was summoned to London where he reasoned with the Crown for a defense plan that would be necessary to protect the growing trade. The more extensive argument was for British rule instead of the rule of the Lord's Proprietors. Charles Towne and the Carolinas were taken back under the protection of the British Crown.[46]

Jack came back. He had kids to raise and a legacy to live out. He was thought to be the most consequential man of the first fifty years of the Carolina Colony. He died in 1724 and is buried under St. Helena's Church. Yes, under! He wasn't buried under it on purpose. The church burned down twice. Upon the last rebuild, the artisans lost the record of where his grave was located. Though a metal marker adorns the old fencing, the grave has been relocated under the existing church.

The man was awesome!

Sunrise at the Atlantic Ocean, Folly Beach. It is
where America wakes up each day.
Photo by author.

CHAPTER 16

Thomas Elfe and the Art of Furniture

WHEN I WAS growing up, I thought of Thomas Elfe as a little guy. I don't know why I thought that. Elfe's handcrafted furniture was his life's work. From 1746 to 1775 he was numero uno, according to most who knew the biz. He was the brightest and best furniture maker in America. His actual height remains unknown.

The thirty years that he made Charleston furniture became a prodigious period. Though most of the furniture remained in Charleston homes, some pieces were shipped across the world. Elfe's celebrated pieces included stacked chests, highboys, tables, cabinets, and sideboards.

Charleston was an English colony still. Elfe was born in London and learned the craft over there before coming here. He was fortunate that when he came to the Holy City, another craftsman took him in. A year later, his mentor-benefactor died. Well, that's actually when he "benefacted." He left all of his materials and tools to Elfe. In time, Elfe hired and trained employees. With a booming economy and plenty of shillings to go around, the Elfe workshop (not Santa's place at the North Pole) was putting out seventeen new pieces per month.[47] Elfe was in high demand.

It is worth noting that his early apprentice contemporary and friend, Thomas Chippendale, was doing quite well during the same period. After Chippendale made a bunch of chairs, he looked for a table. Elfe did tables. The Chippendales are on tour when they are not in Las Vegas. My wife told me that bit of info.

The furniture craft was taught to many of the artisan slave labor force in the 1700s and early 1800s. These plantation pieces were generally built-ins—cabinets and shelves that were measured to fit around a mantle and fireplace or to be emplaced as cupboards in kitchens. Much of this can be seen in the plantation culture, especially at Middleton Place and Drayton Hall.

Source material on Charleston's furnishings from years past has been published because the furniture was opulent. And I quote, "Charleston was the most thoroughly British city outside the British Isles. As the wealthiest city in the country through the end of the eighteenth century, the decorative arts of this cosmopolitan hub reflect the affluence enjoyed by its residents."[48] Thus, I quoted. I could not have said it better.

I don't rightly know who carved the high posts for the rice beds. They became so popular for so long that my wife and I have a reproduction of several earlier reproductions. In theory, the summertime included a set of mesh curtains to keep the mosquitoes drooling on the outside. Later, they moved the mesh to the windows and called them screens. Later yet, they came up with air-conditioning.

By supposition, our furniture was different than the furniture of the hinterlands up Interstate 95. Back then they called that road something else. It was the Snowbound Trail. The Charleston homes had the very best of Charleston-made furnishings.

My granny's home had been in the family for generations (six). The furnishings were astonishing. The oak four-poster bed that my granny utilized moved down several generations. It is a massive structure heavier than three sofas full of people at the bariatric weight-loss center. The mattress and box springs had to be specially crafted. My brother Charlie restored it to its former glory as a project. But now it's too nice to sleep on.

My grandmother's old family home also had a leaf-extended mahogany dining table that could seat sixteen! I often thought that my parents stopped at nine children because sixteen is just ridiculous. But somebody back then thought it was the right number.

These days, few people make hand-made furniture. It's so much easier to go online at Amazon or on the eBay site and pick out something. In a way, quality furniture makes more sense than just about anything. It is an art of function that should last many generations. Well, that is, except for television component cabinets built from the 1970s to the 1990s. They have absolutely no further use at all.

President Washington visited Charleston for
a week in 1791. Photo by author.

CHAPTER 17

George Washington's Horse

JUST A FEW blocks down Ashley Avenue from the little pink house where I grew up, George Washington tied his horse to a tree in 1791. Two hundred years later, the tree was hit by lightning. They had to take it down. They mulched the oaken stump and removed it all. They replaced the excavated area with new soil. Then they planted a new tree so that future generations will honor that the middle of Ashley Avenue has a concrete-curbed and protected site. It's where George Washington tied his horse to a tree replacement. Or it could be a local tall tale. Georgie never confirmed the story and the horse died awhile back.

The father of our country did indeed visit the Holy City on his southern tour during the first week of May (1991).[49] The William Heyward house on Church Street was a proper place to house our first president since we had no Trump Tower. We still don't have a Trump Tower or a tower of any kind.

Poor old William Heyward, a signer of the Declaration of Independence, lost half the naming rights to his own home. The Heyward-Washington House domiciled the Heywards well before and well after Big George. But the "Week of Washington" merited signage for posterity.

Georgie had an evening meal at a tavern named for a son of Mother McCrady. McCrady's Tavern still exists and has a long room for dining upstairs. They call it the Long Room. It's a catchy name. By lore, they ate short ribs.

On another evening, May 4, 1791, there was a meal served at the Exchange Building. Although the more prominent men of Charleston attended, the official count showed that there were 250 women in attendance. Where was Martha? There were a lot of toasts and some serious lady-swooning. Too many toasts upped the swoon count to an unrepeatable number. The prez walked home.

President Washington went over to Fort Moultrie the next day, which was Fort O'Sullivan on Sullivan's Island but not O'Sullivan's Island. He was brought there to inspect the battlements and to hear General Moultrie tell the tale of the battle that had taken place fifteen years before he rode in on his white horse. There, Moultrie told of the harrowing exchange against the warships commanded by British admiral Peter Parker. The famous battle took place six days before the Declaration of Independence was signed. Locally, June 28th is Carolina Day. It's another excuse to skip work and have a parade.

Given that airmail and UPS and such had not been chartered yet, the Declaration of Independence took a long time to get to the British king named George—no relation. You can bet that old guy had a hissy-fit when that parchment arrived.

President Washington probably laughed at Moultrie when he said that he placed palmetto logs along the perimeter of the unfinished fort. It was an emergency option that did not include duct tape. But the palmetto logs worked out well, minimizing the canon fire impact from the twenty-four attacking ships. Even with this evidence and the surprise victory, there has never been a fort built out of palmetto logs since that battle. Engineers have tried silly putty, paper-mâché, and Lincoln Logs, but never went back to using our state tree. Methinks Washington left the island after that crazy story and said to himself, *"Yeah, right!"*

He had to get back to the peninsula soon because four hundred ladies were getting dressed for yet another big party at the St. Cecilia's Society. By conjecture, many were the same ladies from the Exchange Building event but in different dresses. Since George was tall and lanky, they say he turned a mean minuet. Back in Mount Vernon, they called him the Dancing General. But four hundred ladies were a bit much. Paul McCartney didn't get that many screaming fans at his first Liverpool concert. George repowdered his wig and hung in.

He had a few other days of festivities, meals, visits, and official appearances. He went to the new orphanage (which is now the old orphanage) and visited 113 children. This was a city of firsts that included orphanages, libraries, and anything mixed with booze.

Washington had the occasion to raise a toast to Charleston that evening at yet another soiree, and they wrote down every word for posterity—all five of them. He raised his wine goblet and said, "The commercial interests of Charleston!" Canons followed with salutes to his profound and beneficial insight. Years later, Boeing and Volvo moved up off the interstate. How could he have known?

He was invited to multiple church services on Sunday, May 8th. He didn't want to offend anyone, so he accepted both invitations. He attended St. Philips Church in the morning (note the signers to the Declaration and to the U.S. Constitution in their graveyards). Georgie went to St. Michael's for a Sunday afternoon service. It was probably the same biblical reading with nearly the same sermon. Other resident Charleston signers of the U.S. Constitution and Declaration of Independence crowd St. Michael's cemetery. Impressive, huh? Realizing that we were already The Holy City before the American Revolution did not compel our first president to go to services twice on the same Sunday. He did it on his own. Perhaps he had to pray and repent after being chased by hundreds of our most elegant ladies. Martha never received photos or emails of his Charleston activities.

The Charleston mayor (called the warden then), the governor, and other dignitaries saw the president off the next morning. They bid him a genuine Charleston adieu. Washington responded, "Sir, I beg you will accept and offer my best thanks to the corporation and the citizens of Charleston, for their very polite attention to me. Should it ever be in my power, be assured, it will give me pleasure to visit again this very respectable city." He was much more eloquent in leaving than he was at hoisting toasts.

But he never came back—unless that's his ghost up in Room 10 at the B&B.

He visited other plantations on the way to Savannah before returning to his white house at Mt. Vernon. The actual White House was not built, as yet—in the newly planned city of Washington. (It was a Charlestonian, James Hoban, who designed it.) Now, when presidents visit, they come in on Air Force One and tie up the streets and the airports. And they only stay for a few hours, not a week. Too bad they miss all of those cool parties and church services.

That brings us back to Ashley Avenue where George Washington reportedly parked his horse. There is no evidence that he brought a horse to Charleston, but it is not out-of-the-question. He was an excellent horseman. He could've gone for a brisk ride with someone else's horse. There is no evidence that he was asked to tour Ashley Avenue by the hospitals and see the little pink house where the McQueeneys ran around barefooted. Since some of his time was not recorded—like when he bathed or when he slept—then let's just leave that tree on Ashley Avenue within the parameters of his visit. We go through a lot of trouble to make this stuff up.

Charleston's Waterfront Park.
Photo by author.

CHAPTER 18

Oh! Eliza Lucas

MANY OF US would need smelling salts if any of our children wrote us a formal letter thanking us for the privilege of their education. Little Eliza Lucas did just that. She was in a boarding school in England (because colonists were all English citizens in her day). She was not looking for the easy life, a rich husband, or a cache of recipes for her cookbook. She was studying botany.[50]

By 1739, Eliza's mother died, and her father was managing a military conflict in Antigua. As the oldest child, she was overseeing three family plantations here in Charleston. She had not yet turned seventeen.[51] It didn't seem that way then, but it was the break she needed. Her brilliance had a corridor.

Her father was a British colonel and served as lieutenant governor of Antigua. Beyond the military defense of the island, his duties were substantial. Eliza would need to make do (a Geechee expression) on her own. To make do is our way of saying, "persevere," and has nothing to do with walking the dog. Eliza's father knew that Eliza had substantial abilities. He sent her many seeds from Antigua, including several types of indigo plant seeds.

Eliza experimented with combinations of seeds and soil and differing planting seasons. By 1744 she found the right combination. South Carolina had a second money crop behind rice. Wait. You want to know what indigo is, right?

Indigo is a legume plant in the same family as peas. But the plant can produce varieties of dyes, all blue. The dyes are used in the textile industry. Without indigo, most of the early eighteenth-century clothing would have been too bland for women to get dates. Without dating, there would have been a drop off in marriages and fewer children—and we might not have made it into the nineteenth-century. As colors of dyes improved, women started looking much better in their lovely dresses, and we were able to call at least one of them a twentieth-century fox.

Within five years of Eliza Lucas's successful experimentation, indigo became one-third of the export economy of South Carolina. Way to go, Eliza!

Eliza married Charles Pinckney in 1744. She was equally enthralled to be a wife and wrote a letter extolling her new responsibilities.

She vowed "to make a good wife to my dear Husband in all its several branches; to make all my actions Correspond with that sincere love and Duty I bear him. I am resolved to be a good mother to my children, to pray for them, to set them good examples, to give them good advice, to be careful both of their souls and bodies, to watch over their tender minds."[52]

She did just that. Her oldest son Charles Cotesworth Pinckney became a signer of the Declaration of Independence (1776) and a presidential candidate (1796). He donated the city market to the City of Charleston. Her son Thomas negotiated the maritime rights to the Mississippi River from Spain in 1795.[53] Eliza raised some humdinger children.

Eliza Lucas Pinckney died in 1793. She was born in Antigua, schooled in London, managed her family plantations in the British colonial city of Charles Towne, and died in the recently renamed Charleston in the new United States of America.

Wrought Iron Gates, 1963.
Watercolor by Charlotte Simmons McQueeney.

CHAPTER 19

What Has Philip Simmons Wrought?

CHARLESTON OOZES OF fine detail from centuries of artisans. When Philip Simmons passed away in 2009, one of the great Charleston artistic legacies ended. He was the finest metal and iron craftsman the city had ever known. He learned his trade from a former slave.

When Simmons was only eighteen years of age in 1930, an aging blacksmith from his Charleston neighborhood taught him much about metals and temperatures. Peter Simmons (no relation) was born a slave in 1854.[54] He took Philip under his tutelage.

Philip Simmons started out making horseshoes. Over the next seventy-seven years, he adorned Charleston with wrought iron gates, banisters, benches, and archways.

Owing his abilities in the craft to a man who had taught him, Philip Simmons has mentored others along the way. His sense of design was unmatched in the Lowcountry. His genius established, he spent his later years in high demand.

The National Endowment for the Arts bestowed an award to Simmons in 1982. His acceptance speech was indicative of his devotion to the craft.

"My instrument is an <u>anvil</u>. I guess some of you have heard me play... a tune on the anvil, the old blacksmith tune. I'm proud of that anvil, really proud. That anvil fed me when I was hungry, and that anvil clothed me when I was naked. That anvil put shoes on my feet." [55]

Walking the city of Charleston, one would be hard-pressed not to encounter the brilliant artwork of the master craftsman. From High Battery to the Charleston Museum, from the city marina to the South Carolina Aquarium—the artful notions are impressive. There are full balcony rails with distinctive inlaid medallions. He crafted animals and flowers from malleable materials forged in his shop furnace. He'd draw it out and then make it in metal. He had no peer. His eyes and his hands were instruments of inspiration.

The Smithsonian has the work of Philip Simmons, as does the Charleston International Airport and the Charleston Visitor Center.[56] Because of his uniqueness in the world that forges art instead of art forgeries, he is represented in Santa Fe, New Mexico; Atlanta, Georgia; and Columbia, South Carolina (in the Governor's Mansion). And those are only the public places. Most of his metal artwork is owned by private collectors.

In his seventy-seven years as a blacksmith, Simmons never forgot that his work came from sweat and toil. He was proud to put his strength and creativity together in each beat of a hammer that made something different than anything else in that genre. He hammered out a living while forging a legacy.

Foggy sunrise at Patriot's Point. The wildlife slept late.
Photo by author.

Grave of Seminole warrior Osceola. The grave is in front of
Fort Moultrie on Sullivans Island. Photo by author.

CHAPTER 20

Seminole Leader Osceola

E THICS. WE TEACH ethics to our children. But there are others that need these lessons, as well. There are corporations and small businesses, medical professionals, law enforcement, and even church congregations. Ethics apply to all people and the entities they coddle, coerce, and control.

One may be perplexed by a small decision that, if not within the guidelines of fiduciary ethics, will corrupt future decisions. The step-back look is always that, whatever we do, we should be honest and forthright beyond our own personal gain—sometimes even to the point of sacrifice. The accepted basis of decisions made long ago is not impervious to today's public ethics. Ethics are timeless.

Our community has an ethical thorn, and it can be quite prickly.

That old fort on Sullivan's Island named for American Revolutionary war hero William Moultrie has an incredible history. Among its roll call of celebrities who inhabited that bastion guard of our harbor were Francis Marion, Edgar Allan Poe, William Tecumseh Sherman, Abner Doubleday, and even George C. Marshall. It's that other celebrity that is the thorn in the state's ethical core.

Billy Powell was born in the year 1804 at Tallassee, Alabama, of Scots-Irish ancestry with a little English and Native American mix in for good measure. He was part Creek and Muscogee Indian.[57] His mother, Polly Coppinger, was not unlike others of the area—hardened frontier people building a future from the land. His father, William Powell, was an English trader who had earned associations with the Creek Indians.

When Billy Powell was only ten years of age, the Creeks were confronted by none other than Old Hickory himself, General Andrew Jackson. The future president put down a Native American uprising by horrific means—so much so that one of his men, Davy Crockett, became his lifelong adversary. One of his other soldiers was Sam Houston, the first President of the Republic of Texas. But I digress!

After the devastating losses in Alabama to General Jackson's War of 1812 forces, Billy Powell's mother protected the young boy by taking him with the fleeing Creeks to Florida. The Powells had adopted the Creek culture. In time, the young man was given a Creek name, "Osceola," that signified a "shout from a black drink." It was like swallowing the first gulp of dark Guinness Stout in a Dublin pub.

The Creek tribe adopted Osceola, and he eventually rose to become a heroic figure of leadership among the Seminole Tribe of Florida. His refusal to be removed from Florida by the Indian Removal Act of 1832[58] to a reservation west of the Mississippi identified his resolve. He learned guerilla warfare tactics. His subsequent aggression against the forces that would physically remove him and his people brought him the reputation, among the Seminole, as a most valiant warrior. Osceola became their most honored leader.

General Thomas S. Jesup utilized the deception of a white flag and a promise of a new treaty of truce to lure Osceola to meet at a neutral ground. The trusting Osceola walked willingly into the hands of his dishonest captor. This willful misdeed ended the Second Seminole War.

The town of Jesup, Georgia, is named for this Creek and Seminole fighter-general.[59] Perhaps the town founders did not know that General Jesup did not play fair. By any measure, the Jesup name is not a name of military honor. But the "Jesuponians" who live there probably don't know that. Nonetheless, never get in a card game with anyone named Jesup.

Osceola was first taken to St. Augustine (Fort Mason),[60] and then to Fort Moultrie. During his incarceration on Sullivan's Island, the great Seminole leader died of malaria. He was buried just outside of the front entrance to the Revolutionary fort on January 30, 1838. To recap, Osceola was a mostly white citizen born in Alabama who was forced out with his adopted tribe to Florida and was captured dishonorably and brought to South Carolina where he lived less than thirty days. We've kept his remains here for nearly two centuries. His remains are interred within a small iron fence in front of the fort.

The Seminoles want him back where he belongs. Florida wants him back, too. But somewhere along the way, somebody thought that he might bring a tourist or two our way. Some verbal wars between authoritative agencies ensued throughout the interim times. There was even a hoax of theft of Osceola's bones in 1966. It did not occur.

In a similar verbal claim case, the CSS Hunley artifact, a Confederate submarine, belongs here where it made world history and then mysteriously disappeared for 137 years. We found it. Alabama's claim of manufacture fell understandably short of the South Carolina argument of its naval history, crewmembers, and place of demise.

But the case of Osceola is overwhelmingly different. He was never a free man in Charleston, but rather an inmate whisked away from his adopted people. He created no other history here than dying a broken man. He fought no battles here. He had no family here. Everything important that was ever the persona of Osceola was edified and dignified in Florida. He belongs with the Seminole tribe, among those prodigious and proud peoples whose ancestors that he once led. His rightful home is Florida. It's the ethical choice.

Though I have written letters to authorities to right this two-century-old wrong, it does not seem important to them. (My latest correspondence was to Florida Governor Rick Scott.) We need to pull this unethical thorn out of our community. Let's send Osceola back to the lands he once defended. Both Florida and South Carolina will be better for it.

Bust of Henry Timrod at Washington Park. Photo by author.

CHAPTER 21

Literary Charleston

C HARLESTON HAS BEEN blessed in many ways. Authors have risen to prominence from our pluff mud. The literati may have found steroidal inspiration in our city. So many were either born here or spent an inordinate amount of time here doing what they do best—writing.

Before America had its first opera, *Porgy and Bess*, it had DuBose Heyward and *Porgy*. The story was based on reality—a Charleston street vendor named Sammy Smalls. DuBose Heyward was a direct descendant of Thomas Heyward, a Signer of the Declaration of Independence. The book was published in 1925 and the opera in 1935 as a collaboration with George Gershwin. Yeah, he came here, too. Small world, huh?

William Gilmore Simms did not sign any important documents in the founding of America. But Edgar Allan Poe wrote that Simms was the best novelist America ever produced. Simms was more—a novelist, poet, and historian. He once wrote, "He who would acquire fame must not show himself afraid of censure. The dread of censure is the death of genius."[61] It's good that he felt that way because the Charlestonian was deeply censured after the Civil War and he died in 1870 as a nearly forgotten man. He has since been accorded the title as the South's most celebrated author. There remains a lot of competition!

Concurrent with Simms as an author, Henry Timrod (yet another Charlestonian) was deemed as the Poet Laureate of the Confederacy. The singer-songwriter Bob Dylan cites Timrod as a major influence upon his career.[62] Sadly, Timrod's works were delayed in their proper hoist of notoriety. Losing a war does that. He died young and impoverished in 1867.

Another passing had ripples across the literary landscape of Charleston. Modern best-selling author Pat Conroy died in 2016.

Conroy's tales included *The Lords of Discipline, The Great Santini, The Prince of Tides, South of Broad,* and *Beach Music.* Conroy featured a Charleston setting throughout his literary career. He softened up The Citadel's English Department before I arrived. Conroy made me palatable.

The lady authors of Charleston have elevated the art. Alexandra Ripley, Dorothea Benton Frank, and Alice Monroe have all featured the city of their affection in their best-selling careers. I was fortunate to know Dottie Benton from high school and watch in amazement as she published nineteen fabulous books (to date). Her typing fingers have got to be worn slap out!

James O. Rigney, Jr., was a Vietnam veteran (helicopter machine gunner) who graduated from The Citadel with me in 1974. He wrote under the pseudonym "Robert Jordan." Whether he's Jim or "Pseudo Robert," he had the highest contemporary science fiction readership worldwide outside of J.R.R. Tolkien upon his passing in 2007. The *Wheel of Time* series encompassed thirteen books. He also co-wrote the *Conan the Barbarian* series of seven novels. When Jim passed away, I attended his funeral along with so many other family, friends, and admirers. Jim had a heart of gold. An era of magic had passed.

Frank B. Gilbreth, Jr. (1911-2001) wrote *Cheaper by the Dozen* and made Charleston his home. His local columns made us laugh at ourselves. He was a personal favorite because he made hilarious fun of the Geechee-Gullah culture. I certainly identified with his comical insights and recognized that my verbs confused folks even more than my nouns.

Though we are most definitely Geechees, make no mistake. The writers in Charleston are verdant. We may not be able to say the words in a particular order or sound that is readily understood by the masses, but the amused New York editors make us sound brilliant!

Singer-songwriter Darius Rucker is a native Charlestonian
and among the most charitable of celebrities.
Photo by author.

CHAPTER 22

Celebrity Convergences

AFTER *THE ADVENTURE* landed in 1670, Charlestonians looked around to see if they spotted anyone familiar wearing dark sunglasses. Ever since then, we have had a habit of spotting celebrities. Some even live here!

What makes a celebrity? There are many channels. There are musicians, talk show hosts, politicians, models, sports figures, actors, comedians, religious leaders, authors, top executives, and the filthy rich. Yes, I've struck out on all counts.

By now, most people know that actor-comedian Bill Murray lives here. I have his cellphone number, but he told me that if I ever call it, he'd have to change it. Although Murray is from the Chicago area (Wilmette, Illinois), he belongs here. He gets the Charleston culture and extends the welcome further than anyone.

Charleston has native-born celebrities, as well. Darius Rucker, Lauren Hutton, and Art Shell number among our most distinguished progeny. Add in Stephen Colbert, Thomas Gibson, Jimmy Byrnes, Fritz Hollings and Governor James B. Edwards. Congressman Joe Wilson ("You lie!") has a seat in the U.S. Congress but is from Charleston. He just got a little excited, I suppose. LPGA Hall-of-Famer Beth Daniel is a native daughter.

U.S. House members Tommy Hartnett, L. Mendel Rivers, Arthur Ravenel, Jr., and Henry Brown were born here. United States Senator Tim Scott is also from Charleston.

Among Charleston's native sons, the genius of the class was inventor-entrepreneur Jerry Zucker (1949-2008). Zucker founded the InterTech Group and owned over 150 international companies including Canada's largest and oldest retailer, the Hudson Bay Company. His family remains the epitome of patronage to public educational enhancements.

One of the seventy-one living Medal of Honor recipients calls Charleston home. Major General James E. Livingston, USMC Retired, earned his citation for extreme valor in the face of overwhelming odds. The 1968 Battle of Dai Do was conducted as a surprise to both factions. The three hundred or so U.S. Marines did not expect that they were taking on a major Viet Cong offensive of 10,000 men. The Viet Cong had no idea that such a small force was stymieing them. General Livingston's bravery in this conflict is legendary.

Nearly one hundred retired military flag officers live in the area. These are the admirals and generals that like the pace of life near the palmettos.

Our illustrious past also includes Joel Roberts Poinsett, physician and diplomat, who brought the world the Christmas poinsettia; architect Robert Mills designed the Washington Monument; Charlestonian James Hoban, who, not to be outdone, designed the White House; Denmark Vesey, who was a freed slave who led an uprising in Charleston; and World War II General Mark W. Clark, who was president of The Citadel and is buried on the campus of the military college.

Sports stars? Yeah. We got 'em. Harold Green, David Meggett, Roddy White, Carlos Dunlap, Zola Davis, Luther Broughton, Oronde Gadsden, Langston Moore, Ovie Mughelli, A.J. Green, and Robert Quinn plied their skills in the National Football League. Laron Profit, Anthony Johnson, Kwame Brown, Josh Powell and Khris Middleton became NBA players of distinction. Katrina McClain was an Olympic gold medalist and retired from the WNBA. Bud Moore had to get through the northbound traffic on Interstate 26 to earn his standing in NASCAR.

Others have moved here. Some have homes or had homes in the area. Coaches? Roy Williams, Ralph Friedgen, Les Robinson, Bobby Cremins, Fisher DeBerry, Tom O'Brien, Bobby Johnson, Cal McCombs, Paul Scarpa, Frank Navarro, Dan Carnevale, and Oliver Purnell. ESPN broadcaster Debbie Antonelli lives here. Other former NFL players live here—Dan Marino, Ed Marinaro, and Jim Stuckey. You'll also find Olympian Tara Lipinski, NASCAR owner Joe Gibbs, and actress Reese Witherspoon. Pittsburgh Steelers quarterback Ben Roethlisberger likes it here. He owns the King Street Grille.

We do not have a Pluff Mud walk-of-fame to check out, but a visitor should not be surprised to see Oprah Winfrey or Bill Gates roaming our streets. Charleston is among their most favored destinations.

Although it is wise to look down often enough not to trip on our uneven sidewalks, look up and around. You'll either see someone or they'll see you!

STONES, BONES, AND GROANS

Charleston Street Scene. Watercolor by Charlotte Simmons McQueeney.

CHAPTER 23

In Sunshine or Rain

LET'S SUPPOSE THAT the sun is out and the breezes are plentiful. You wouldn't sit in your hotel room and watch Judge Judy. You would join the living and tour Charleston with the excitement of a school child on a field trip. It's where you could spot a Geechee geechinating.

With time allotted upon a generous schedule, you would see Fort Sumter, the High Battery (White Point Gardens), the City Market area, a half-dozen museums, a few graveyards, and Washington Park. You'd zip right on to the Four Corners of Law. Walk a block back down Meeting Street, and you see Chalmers Street full of cobblestones, the Pink House, and the Old Slave Mart Museum. Circle back to the Circular Congregational Church and the Hibernian Society Hall. Drift over to the Old Jail (Magazine Street), the newly renovated Colonial Lake (still full of old water), and Randolph Hall at the College of Charleston. Thank heavens you don't need to buy film and reload a camera along the way!

A tour of The Citadel is time well spent. I recommend visiting the new Citadel War Memorial and Summerall Chapel. The chapel is uni-denominational. All are welcome.

You might take a full day to see the gardens—in Charleston that means Magnolia Gardens and Middleton Place. But Drayton Hall is right there. It's a must-see. You might cross the river over to Mount Pleasant to see Boone Hall Plantation.

The Yorktown aircraft carrier at Patriots Point gives you a great photo setting for the low profile of the city. While that close, have lunch or dinner at Shem Creek. Load up on She Crab Soup. Avoid the He-Crabby waiter. You could even run over to Sullivan's Island and tour Fort Moultrie.

I would even recommend the Folly Beach Pier. It's just like the ones in California at Huntington Beach and Santa Monica, only smaller and full of Geechees. It's the very best place in the Lowcountry to get a cup of coffee and welcome the morning sunrise airmailed overnight from Europe.

Even if it's cloudy, baseball season goes on. The experience of seeing the Charleston RiverDogs in the best minor league park in baseball (New York Yankee affiliate) cannot be denied. They give you nine full innings of entertainment to include a bat-retrieving Golden Retriever.

You'll find these places in any tourist information center, at the concierge desk, or on the Internet. With the sun out, there is much to explore. The simple joy of walking about the Charleston peninsula is its own reward. There are new interests at every turn.

Walk up the Arthur Ravenel, Jr., Bridge. You can walk up to the wide (15-feet-wide) lane with panoramic views of the harbor, Mount Pleasant, and all of Geechee Land. It's free!

The professional tour guides are wholeheartedly endorsed here as long as they can mispronounce enough words to qualify. Walking across Charleston is a memory in the making. Comfy shoes are a must.

But suppose the outdoor weather is not cooperative. What now? An itinerary would change, but the plan of enjoyment would be just as well enhanced.

Check out the churches. You know St. Michael's and St. Philip's. St. Michael's has the oldest tower clock in North America.[63] Those quarter, half, and hourly chimes should sound familiar. They are the St. Michael's setting on your grandfather clock. The earth-toned St. Philip's Church is perhaps the most photographed church in the state, if not the South.

The churches on the peninsula are unique, stylish, and historical. They are usually open to visitors. Just down Meeting Street from St. Michael's is the First Scots Presbyterian Church. Or try the Second Scots Presbyterian Church further down the same street two blocks north of Calhoun Street. These churches are exactly what they are named. All other U.S. Presbyterian churches came later.

The French Huguenot Church a half block from St. Philip's and it's highly ornamented (Gothic). Think sand castle.

The Cathedral of St. John the Baptist (Broad Street) or the oldest Catholic Church in the Carolinas (St. Mary's on Hasell Street) are entirely different examples of the Roman Catholic influence.

The Mother Emanuel Church on Calhoun Street earned much-storied history before the tragedy of the Charleston Massacre of 2015. It represents a special place for many generations. My friend, Reverend Anthony B. Thompson, tragically lost his wife Myra in the shooting. He honored me by allowing me to speak in the church at the one-year memorial of the horrific loss of nine Charlestonians.

The Unitarian Church on Archdale Street is the second-oldest church in the city.[64] The Grace Church on Wentworth Street has a very popular local congregation.

The Kahal Kadosh Beth Elohim synagogue houses the oldest continuous Jewish congregation in America (Hasell Street). In fact, the words translate as "Holy Congregation House of God."[65] The congregation first assembled in 1749, but a few members have died off since.

The Greek Orthodox Church of the Holy Trinity on Race Street is not old (1953) but is an interesting addition to Charleston's architectural identity. The Bethel United Methodist Church at Pitt Street and Calhoun Street was purchased as a burial ground, but a church was built there in 1795. It's got old bones.

The First Baptist Church (built 1822) is tucked away on Church Street and was a design of the Charleston architect, Robert Mills. He also designed Charleston City Hall and the Washington Monument. Yes, that 555-foot obelisk in Washington, D.C. He could not have planned such a monstrosity in Charleston!

St. Matthew's Lutheran Church (King Street) no longer has repairs ongoing so you can go in. Its steeple, at 255 feet,[66] made it the tallest building in South Carolina for many years. The zoning board uses the church height as a barometer for height on the peninsula, though they would likely deny it. No building has ever exceeded its height.

The public buildings are waiting for you. The Old Exchange Building and Provost Dungeon at the foot of Broad Street is the last British-built public building constructed in America (1771).[67] Note the dungeon! They do tours so that you can see where our captured pirates were chained. The Powder Magazine on Cumberland Street is the oldest public structure in Charleston (1713). They do tours, too. Even the 1911 Peoples building has an interesting history. It hosted President William Howard Taft and sported the state's first elevator. Only nine stories high, it is Charleston's first skyscraper.

The U.S. Custom's House at the end of the City Market looks like it's one of the treasury buildings in Washington, but we kept it anyway. The Charleston Museum on Meeting Street is a newer building with really old things. I put some stuff in there myself. Straight across the street is the old railroad barn that was torn down and rebuilt to look like an old railroad barn. It's now the Charleston Visitor Center. It has an award-winning film about Charleston.

Most of the City Market is rainproof so you can shop dry until you're cash-dry. The Market Hall above it is also still rainproof until the next hurricane. If you see this book in the City Market, buy it. It will keep me from becoming a Pest-Selling author.

Generally, you can peek inside the Dock Street Theater. Just don't stay or they'll make you sweep the lobby. The J. Palmer Gaillard Center was recently completed with a few of the materials left over from the old Gaillard Municipal Auditorium. They didn't save much. It cost $142 million.

Check out the Historic Charleston Foundation Shop on Meeting Street across from the Hibernian Society Hall. Ask the manager to stock more of the book you're reading. It's a subtle marketing ploy I'm trying to advance.

The South Carolina Aquarium was controversial in its infancy because of costs. I sensed that it would be as then-Mayor Joe Riley had planned—an important augmentation to everything else in Charleston. One cannot deny the benefit of laughter as the school children enjoy the playfulness of the otters.

If you have some rumpled clothes that need to be washed and the weather is still a drizzling mess, don't fret. Put them on and head on out the hotel's main entrance without the umbrella and dance wildly in the raindrops. We Geechees do that all the time. It's a tradition. It says, "I love Charleston."

Ashley River Bridges from West Ashley.
Photo by author.

CHAPTER 24

Bridges Become Us

A WALK AROUND the Holy City from the 1950s and 1960s would have been unencumbered by the trepidation of immensity. The walk from the Ashley River to the Cooper River at the peninsula's widest point measures a mile-and-a-half. That widest point is at Calhoun Street. From the tip of the Battery—also cited as White Point Gardens because of its oyster shell paths—to Huger Street measures one-and-three-quarter miles. Not many Charlestonians lived above Huger Street in the 1950s and 1960s.

One could walk across the Ashley River Bridge. The first Ashley River Bridge opened in 1926. The Seth Raynor designed Country Club of Charleston golf course was completed in 1925 near Wappoo Cut on James Island. The likely patrons from downtown Charleston refused to swim to the new course toting a golf bag.

There were few reasons to walk into the West of the Ashley area in the 1950s. The West Ashley component of Charleston's slow growth was comprised of a few scant neighborhoods, a dairy, a few churches, and some of the old South's magnificent formal gardens. There were several farms, as well. One wouldn't walk to Middleton Place or Magnolia Gardens because of the extended distance. Nonetheless, these two gorgeous plantations became Charleston's most significant tourist destinations for many years. Even General Sherman wouldn't dare destroy the magnificent live oaks and color-wheel kaleidoscope of flowers. Ah, nature!

There remains a six-hundred-acre historic site up the Ashley River designated as Charles Towne Landing. It's called that because that's exactly what it is—or was in 1670. It was the first location of Charleston before the settlers decided that the peninsula was more defensible. Besides, there were fewer mosquitos at White Point Gardens. The settlers slowly moved (over the next ten years) to the current peninsula site. Charles Towne Landing eventually became a zoo with bison, alligators, and puma. The puma and the bison left for better pastures, but the alligators multiplied and horrified. Don't walk Skippy, the poodle near the gators.

Since the Silas N. Pearman Bridge was not completed until 1966, only those seeking suicide by fear would challenge a walk across the Grace Memorial Bridge (completed 1929). The Grace Bridge was a roller coaster frequented daily by unsuspecting amateur motorists. Two narrow nine-foot lanes moved traffic in opposite directions north and south. The bridge gained a treacherous reputation—so much so—that most north-south vehicular traffic routed twenty miles west through Summerville. The Grace Bridge became the city's major deterrent to tourism. It supplanted ferryboats. It was finally demolished in 2005.

A bridge was built to accommodate traffic to the Charleston Naval Shipyard from the West Ashley area. It was near the time of the Second World War. But the bridge was so ugly and dull that no bridge builder would take credit, and no municipality would claim it. The bridge has never gained accolades of any type, even though it was erected more than seventy years ago. Usually, the name of the overpaid highway department chairman who builds ugly bridges has his surname emplaced on structures such as the North Ashley River Bridge. This particular honor may have been hidden by the weeds at the approach. The bridge was built as a fixed span to connect a northern part of the peninsula (eventually North Charleston) with West Ashley. It's been called the Northbridge ever since. It's utilitarian and serviceable. But don't go there in the daytime. It's really, really ugly.

Other bridges arrived when a semi-circle of a federal highway was developed. Politicians have been squabbling about that project (Interstate 526) since the discovery of shaved ice. The one that connects North Charleston to the marsh that precedes Daniel Island is called the Don Holt Bridge. Nowadays, it's mostly a parking lot with engines running.

There is also the Wando Bridge (named for former Governor James B. Edwards). This bridge has chartered a most difficult history. Continual inspections turn up continual design flaws. By the spring of 2018, traffic leaving Mt. Pleasant to Daniel Island was halted for emergency repairs that would last more than a month. It snarled the entire Lowcountry.

The neatest bridges are the little ones. The Wappoo Bridge and the Ben Sawyer Bridge are showstoppers. They stop the show when water traffic assembles in the waterways. Sometimes they get stuck. Sometimes they don't. If you happen to be in a tremendous hurry, order a helicopter transport. These draw and swing bridges seem to anticipate anyone in a hurry. That's when they fail.

One of the most magnificent views in America is the panorama gained by reaching the apex of the Isle of Palms Connector Bridge. Since the IOP is rather narrow, the view takes in the Intracoastal Waterway and the waves of the Atlantic smashing into the East Coast. You can walk this bridge or ride your bicycle. My wife once raced me to the top of the bridge riding a bicycle. I haven't seen her in years.

When you see photos of Charleston from elsewhere, the prominent structure is the Arthur Ravenel, Jr., Bridge (opened 2005). It looks the same when you see it in photos here. I once went to the very top of the tower as if I was allowed to change the warning light bulb for airplanes. Of course, it was by a special invitation, and I had to wear a reflective safety vest and a hard hat. I was shoehorned into a slanted and caged elevator traveling slightly inward and backward. Weird! We exited to a fully enclosed concrete room with a steel ladder. The ladder led up another fifteen feet to the hatch. When I emerged from the hatch and looked out, I think I saw Ireland. I stood at 572 feet and looked around to wave at anyone I might know in the river below. Those little dots would not have known I was up there. But my cell phone reception was fantastic. The view to the peninsula and beyond was indescribable. I doubt that there have been a hundred people up there in the dozen years since it was completed, so I felt very privileged. The quickest way back down was a leap, but I decided to take the caged elevator instead.

On that same day when I went to the highest place in the city, I had also been in the sewers. No, really. There was no sewer in the sewers because they were building a new sixty-six-inch pipe connection fifty-five feet under Charleston. We (the head engineer and other guests) were in the thickened marl. By my calculations, I went to the highest and lowest of Charleston in a day—627 feet total under and over. Upon making this verbal claim, I was reminded by a friend that he matched me by going to the Charleston Symphony Orchestra concert and Big John's (old rickety bar with pub food) the same evening. In a different way, he won.

Back to the Ravenel Bridge. It's indeed a modern wonder. It was engineered for hurricanes, earthquakes, and runaway container ships. It has a magnificent fifteen-foot-wide pedestrian and bicycle lane. The city's best female joggers are seen there daily. They have the city's best female jogging outfits, too. Wrecks happen.

The Ravenel Bridge effectively tied the Town of Mount Pleasant to the city of Charleston with a landmark structure. The previous bridge trepidation was removed when they dynamited the older bridges. Subsequently, sleepy Mount Pleasant became the fourth largest city in the state. The Cooper River Bridge Run grew as well. It is among the largest 10K races in America and attracts nearly forty-thousand runners and walkers each year. I jog-walked it in the 2001 race carrying my two-week-old son—born two Saturdays prior. He had his own race number. As far as I know, he is the youngest finisher of the race ever. He had a little help.

Other bridges like the John's Island Bridge and the Scarborough Bridge to James Island are recent as well. The Scarborough Bridge transports people from compacted Calhoun Street gridlock to Folly Road gridlock daily. But it features an outstanding view of the area's largest sewerage treatment plant. No politician has come forward to be honored by the treatment plant naming rights.

The John's Island Bridge is an engineering marvel. It takes unsuspecting vacationers to Kiawah and Seabrook Islands under extreme duress. The wide modern roadway swoops down across the Folly River to a two-lane road (one each way) that leads to a traffic light a mile further down. That one traffic light, at the intersection of River Road and Maybank Highway, backs up traffic for several miles twice a day. Perhaps the brilliant engineer will be brought up on treasonous charges and publicly ridiculed at the Fresh Farms Market that divides Kiawah and Seabrook islands. But no one would be likely to get there in time to enjoy the festivities because of the daily traffic snarl.

The Lowcountry is dependent upon serpentine movement of vehicular traffic in a safe and timely manner. But the challenge is substantial. It's because our rivers and creeks have no morals. They are apt to change beds.

Sometimes the Charleston streets provide transportation
for other touring families. Photo by author.

CHAPTER 25

Which Downtown Streets Flood?

A LL OF THEM. Next question.

Flooding in Charleston started in the Pleistocene era. It was when there was no pleis to be seen.

The topographical charts of the area are cataloged by the Federal Emergency Management Agency (FEMA). This conduit allows that Charleston homeowners can pay a fortune for flood insurance because the banks require it if the homes are mortgaged. But when the storms subside, and the houses have damage, the adjusters stay away because they can't get through the flooded streets.

A birds-eye view of the peninsula would find a few high spots where a full moon high tide would not likely flood the street. Among the most prominent peninsula locations where this condition still exists is Rainbow Row. That topography is high for Charleston. But the polar ice cap could melt away any day now. In that circumstance, the best place near the city to avoid flooding would be our suburb of Columbia.

It is possible that the original settlers noted that the flooding made Charles Towne precarious. But the shrimping was so much easier in their own backyard. The early settlers didn't have the Battery wall to keep the harbor out in the harbor, or pump stations to move the water someplace else.

About the new zillion-dollar pump engineering—the City of Charleston has invested in a European pump system so that your European import automobile will not drown in the high tide. The five-phase pump project will be completed by 2022. Flooding is guaranteed to become a thing of the past then. Right? Not!

I'm a Geechee simpleton, but I've got to ask one of the engineers a question that's been bothering me. Since the need to move the water from the streets is usually at a full moon high tide with a rainstorm, where are we pumping the water? Mount Pleasant? Holly Hill? Singapore? Will it not come back up as other water where the pumped water was displaced? Help me here.

Since engineering is not my forte, I hesitate to offer a permanent solution. Oh, what the hay. I have the answer. We raise the streets.

Yeah. Raise 'em up. We can do it with oversized Legos. Just snap a million one-foot indestructible plastic blocks into place to the height needed. Pop 'em in everywhere—the Crosstown, the Market, by the hospitals—and leave them up year-round. If the tides get worse, just add another Lego-layer. We can do them in Rainbow Row pastel colors or make 'em all charcoal gray to look like the rest of the streets. We could put cobblestone designs on top to give them even more character. The Lego people could do this at prices much lower than those water pump folks from Europe.

Charleston could land another first. We could be the first city in the world with Lego streets. They don't even do Lego streets in Legoland.

View of Broad Street, the city's historical financial center.
Photo by author.

CHAPTER 26

Reversing the Lanes

AMONG OUR MOST recent exercise in questionable administrative judgment is the enactment of reversing lanes on one-way streets. It seems that someone in a boardroom felt that the gridlock was not forming fast enough. Let's investigate.

The downtown area was laid out circa 1680. A map of the orderliness exists today. That 1703 map shows the plan inside the walls. Yes, it was a walled city—the only British walled city in North America. The Spanish already had a walled city—St. Augustine. It was deemed to be too close for comfort. The French had built walled cities, as well—Quebec and Montreal. The essential southern port to the British colonies needed protection. The wall had turreted corners called bastions. These points helped to keep the alligators from attacking.

Within a few decades, our fledgling city by the sea was growing too fast to keep up. The walls were not built far enough apart to quarter the population. Somebody came to the lord mayor at some point and said, "Mr. Gorbachev, tear down this wall." The mayor's name was maybe spelled different then, but the sentiment was the same. Although they tore down the wall, remnants remain. Don't trip on the one at Marion Square.

The teardown allowed for expansion. We could stable the horses, pen in the pigs, and cage the chickens. The streets were just the right width for the horse carriages, except for a few boulevard-like thoroughfares. The houses were built to huddle together as another protection from windstorms. Those streets were narrow, and the traffic was routed accordingly. The wide streets allowed two-way traffic; the narrow ones were one-way. Even the horses knew this plan. There was hardly room on some of these for bicycles because they hadn't been invented yet.

As we grew our total auto population to four vehicles (1906), the traffic plan was put to the test. My great-grandfather was one of four doctors who ordered a car from Indianapolis that was delivered by train in 1906. All were Maxwells—three painted black and one painted white. An unmarried doctor bought the white Maxwell. It made the single women of 1906 Charleston blush.

The city turned out to see the new contraptions unloaded from the train. None of the doctors knew how to drive, and there was no such thing as a driver's license. So, who drove them? They came with instructions and the same carriage drivers who chauffeured the doctors on their rounds learned to operate the new Maxwells. My great-grandfather's family could show off just by riding to church.

The street directions didn't change, but the street signs did. The city placed new stop signs in the middle of intersections because these cars could reach nearly twenty miles per hour. With four of them roaming the streets and polluting the air, all precautions were taken. The Geechees had moved into the motorized era.

The streets remained the same for a hundred years. Ashley Avenue moved one-way north. Spring Street moved one-way west. Cannon Street moved one-way east. Rutledge Avenue moved one-way south. Everybody was happy. Then, the brilliant city engineers got involved because tourists and Uber drivers were turning the wrong way. They decided to make every turn the right direction. After all, as the adage suggests, two wrongs do not make a right but three rights do make a left.

Streets we knew as pristine and pastoral became collision zones. To make matters worse, some of these streets remained one-way for part of the street, then two-way for other sections. Geechees had to re-learn their instincts. My particular instincts are warmed over.

Other streets were impacted—King Street, Wentworth Street, and Beaufain (BEW-fain) Street. All three of these major city streets have functions of two-way traffic that meet a point where there is one-way traffic. Go figure. It made it difficult to tell a visiting downtown driver which way to go. Perhaps GPS will save us. My great-grandfather would have been appalled, but he was already a back-seat driver.

The Mills House was razed and then rebuilt in 1970.
Downtown hotels have high occupancy year-round. Photo by author.

CHAPTER 27

Hotel Mania

THEY SAY WE'RE drawing in more than six million visitors a year to our downtown hotels. It's a 50 percent increase over the four million visitors who stayed in our hotels in 2011. I'm down with that.

They're not sleeping at my house. My wife would have a conniption. For the record, I have never seen a real live conniption.

Hotels are growing out of the pile-driven soil like mushrooms in a wet and shaded field. The skyline has the knitting tools—high cranes competing with our church steeples. When will it ever end? Actually, I kinda like it. Not all Geechees will admit that. I helped erect scaffolding for Ruscon Construction Company in 1970 when the Mills House Hotel was being built. It gave Charleston its first upper-scale hotel with central air-conditioning. It also gave me enough minimum wage earnings to assist my struggling parents and land me in college at The Citadel.

On any particular day in downtown Charleston, nearly 33,000 hotel guests and support staff flood into the peninsula. Figure in room cleaning, bartenders, chefs, wait staff, front-deskateers, and others. Some of the hotels have had to become parking garages with a hotel built around it. My take on that eye-popping number of added daily downtowners is that it's a good thing. They eat lunch, buy things, go on tours, and rent bicycles. The boom to the economy—to me—is worth the congestion.

Hotels could be better than other uses. For instance, hotel traffic is far less than traffic for offices or our hospitals. People in hotels usually walk, bike, or taxi to other locations. Few get rental cars, especially given the compact nature of the downtown area. Fortunately, we have balmy weather and minuscule crime. So, walking presents very little trepidation on behalf of the traveler. The most significant hindrance to the walking tourist may be our uneven sidewalks. How uneven? Think military obstacle course.

The blue slate sidewalks that were laid many moons ago came from Pennsylvania. They used the same material for roofing. Water rolls down slate without penetration. Besides, a massive hurricane cannot move the slate from a roof as it would ordinary shingles. The availability of slate made it convenient to utilize as sidewalks. So what changed? Nature. Our live oaks, crape myrtles, and palmettos got larger. Their root systems expanded. Slate is no match for a live oak root. The joints rose inch by inch. Some cracked in the middle. Patching slate with concrete was a temporary fix. It was destined to crack over and over again. Always beware of Charleston sidewalks! It's covered in another chapter, as well. I did that in case you weren't paying attention.

New hotels brought in fresh new sidewalks and permanent plantings. It may take a full century before tourists trip in front of the new hotels. But beware as they encroach the Old World charm.

New hotels bring in needed ambiance. The city of Charleston is not permitting any cookie-cutter edifices to take up our precious viewing corridors. These hotels may be a part of a national chain, but they are conforming to an upper-end demand for excellence. The style and experience of Charleston are enhanced by the additions. Think five-star luxury. We're getting that. They ooze in our culture with brass, marble, mahogany, and granite. They are built for the duration, unlike our past dalliances with pizza chains and car dealerships. Besides, every upscale hotel that I have encountered in my away-travels leaves an excellent impression. It could be the pool, the bar, or the breakfast menu. They deliver added character.

A walk through without tripping would find some colossal hotel success stories. The Old Citadel (1842-1922) was converted to an Embassy Suites Hotel twenty years ago. It's an amazing property. Facing the same public square, a ragged old federal office building became the stately Dewberry. Another new kid on the block will be the Bennett Hotel (due to open in late 2018). The Bennett Hotel may redefine luxury in Charleston.

The Harbour View Inn near Waterfront Park is excellently located and well appointed. There is even a newer Charleston version of an upscale Holiday Inn on Meeting Street. It just ain't the Holiday Inn we knew.

The Restoration Inn was named the best new hotel in Charleston. The Grand Bohemian and The Spectator push the star charts far to the right. The Market Street Pavilion and the French Quarter Inn are exquisite properties near the city market. Great other choices include the Planters Inn, The Belmond (grand-daddy of the best when it opened in 1986), and the Wentworth Mansion. There's a new Hilton and a new Hyatt. Take your pick. Both are right.

I wish I had seen this hotelier industry coming and invested on the ground floor of one of these stoic and attractive additions. I might have earned naming rights. My new hotel would have had a perfect name to add new Charleston visitors via the Internet. Whadaya think of "The Hotel Conniption?" Catchy, huh?

Architectural styles are opulent and classical.
Photo by author.

CHAPTER 28

Hark the Architecture

OTHER THAN THE cannon balls, bullet holes, earthquake cracks, and smoke stains, the remaining architecture of America's most historic city lauds much of the Old World. It's difficult to find anything less than a hundred years old on the peninsula, with the exception of the Harris Teeter supermarket.

Unlike other cities that were built during a thrush of growth from a condensed period of style, Charleston evolved over centuries. There are definitive growing periods related to economics, but they did not alter the character of the cityscape. It's because there are periods of no growth. We called it "destitution." Mind you, it happened.

The prominent residential style is the Charleston single house. They did not get that designation because of the single people who could not get a date who lived there. It's because the living quarters are a single room wide. Some conjecture exists that they were built narrow because the lots would be taxed by the street footage. That was never the case. The construction made sense because of the Charleston heat and humidity.

The Charleston ceiling heights back then were usually at thirteen feet—to control the humidity by giving the heat a place to collect up high. The second story would have high ceilings, as well. Some old Charleston edifices even have a "cupola." We had these before Francis Ford "Cupola" was born. A cupola dome is a glass abruption on the roof that collects the house heat to be dispersed by opening its windows. It was an early form of air-conditioning.

The single house typically has side porches on both floors on the southeast side to catch the prevailing breezes. We call these piazzas. In Italy, a piazza would be a large public square. In Charleston, it's a private open rectangle. It's the best room in the house that's not in the house.

A single house's windows are large and shuttered. The size is for the breeze. The shutters are for the big, big, breeze. They are a planned feature because we plan to have hurricanes. I shudder to mention them, but they're part of who we are—a resilient bunch.

A Charleston double house is the same as saying a Charleston mansion. These are two rooms wide with all of the same features as the single house, but with more furniture. Double houses are generally on large lots with gardens, water features, and a carriage house.

A carriage house was not only a place for a carriage but a stable, as well. Now, they are called names like a "dependency" or a "separate quarters." Most of these have been converted to opulent Charleston addresses that have the main house number with a half added. Don't be surprised if you see a carriage house on the market and the price is seven figures. The ground beneath them is well fertilized.

Note that a proper Charleston single house or double house (mansion) has no windows on the north or west side. It is the result of a stilted homage to decency. Our neighbor's piazzas were there. No windows gave the neighbors their cherished privacy. The only way to be a Peeping Tom was to climb up into the extraordinary heat of the roof cupola.

Some homes were borne of a European or Caribbean style. You can find lovely examples of Queen Anne, Tudor, Georgian, and Colonial architecture. There are Federal, Adamesque, Italianate, French Provincial, and Victorian. Rainbow Row has a Dutch flair. The high battery has everything from Greek Revival to Art Deco.

Our commercial and public buildings are a different story. They are large and robust with even more refinement. You'll see hand-carved woodwork and free-standing stairways. Materials are marble, granite, and even a cedar house carved to look like stone blocks. The roofing is usually comprised of slate panels. That had to be some roofing contractor!

Even in the churches, we see the architectural character. You can find Gothic, Palladian, Colonial, Baroque, and Romanesque. I can tell you which is which, but you'll need to let me know where to meet you. The Circular Congregational Church on Meeting Street was built to be reminiscent of the Pantheon in Rome. Our churches gave us our reputation. But we never seem to spend enough time there.

Though many materials are used across the peninsula because the port trade made them available, the proper use of the materials became the focus. Designs are stunning. Artisans with special abilities produced styles as simple as the Flemish bond seen in our Charleston brick walls and window lentils. The distinctive brickwork is especially evident in the old Charleston double-houses.

Look up, down, and all around. You are walking through one of the finest museums of classical architecture in America. We were too poor to tear anything down. It was a blessing.

The USS Yorktown serves as a reminder of
Charleston's extensive military history.
The massive ship once housed 5000 sailors.
Photo by author.

CHAPTER 29

Military Affiliations

NEAR THE TIME of Charleston's settlement in 1670, the world was in a constant abrasive mentality. The Dutch were fighting the Swedes. The Swedes were fighting the Danes, the Russians, and the Norwegians. The Ukrainians were fighting the Polish and the Lithuanians. Even the Tibetans were at war—with the Ladahks of India. And the Holy Roman Empire went to war with the Ottoman Turks yet again.[68]

It is no wonder that military presence in Charleston—as well as the rest of America—was essential. It was the same way in our large family. If you wanted to keep something, you had to be willing to fight for it.

Charleston's first fort was where Charleston first was. See the replica fort at Charles Towne Landing. Since then, we have improved the science of the military defenses quite a bit. At one time we had all five services in Charleston.

The Coast Guard Base at Charleston started at Sullivan's Island in 1891. It moved to eight acres at what we Charlestonians call Low Battery in 1914. Low Battery was here well before the modern cellphone indicated the same term.

The Charleston Coast Guard Base was initially a buoy depot, as well. The Coast Guard station is now a vital part of the community and an integral part of both Charleston's defense and search-and-rescue missions.

The U. S. Army commitment to Charleston pre-dates America. The U.S. Army built forts along the southeast coast. Fort Sumter (now a monument) was part of that effort. Fort Moultrie was initially Fort O'Sullivan and dealt Britain the most significant naval defeat of the American Revolution. It was rebuilt in 1798 in response to another war between Britain and France. Much of it suffered damage in an 1804 hurricane. The fort was used sporadically until the breakout of World

War I when it was garrisoned with artillery. It was again garrisoned with larger artillery in 1939 in anticipation of World War II. The army lowered the flag at Fort Moultrie for the last time in 1947 after 171 years of service. In 1960, the abandoned fort was transferred to the National Park Service.[69] The Army has had other presence in Charleston including the U. S. Army Air Corps and a U.S. Army recruiting center.

The United States Navy had a presence in Charleston from 1901 to 1996. Some civilian support commands still exist in North Charleston to include the Southern Naval Facilities Engineering Command (South NavFac) and a naval electronics component (Navalex). Submarines were a well-established part of the large—and now empty—navy base. At the present, some progressive makeovers are in evidence at the site. There is a new training center for Homeland Security.

Besides Parris Island in Beaufort, the United States Marine Corps has maintained a weapons depot near Goose Creek since 1941. They call it the Naval Weapons Station, not to be confused with the U.S. naval weapons because the United States Marine Corps uses naval weapons, as well. Never knock on the door and ask for directions to the nine-hole golf course. I did that once, and the armed guard assumed I was a spy. My Geechee tones saved me from certain torture.

The United States Air Force was the U.S. Army Air Corps until the National Security Act of 1947.[70] The flyboys finally got their own budget, traditions, and uniforms. One would be uninformed to not consider the Charleston Air Force Base, now part of Joint Base Charleston, to be an integral part of the community. It is the primary worldwide base for the military's largest transport plane, the C-17. These incredible planes could have made transporting the P.T. Barnum and Bailey Circus an easy exercise no matter how many elephants were in the Big Top.

It's a fact that Charleston has enjoyed a long historical and strategic role in the history of the United States military. It is also a fact that the Charleston Coast Guard Base used to sell case beer to any ROTC student at discount pricing. Another benefit was accorded to Air Force ROTC students. They could take dates on Friday nights to the Officers Club on the Charleston Air Force Base and buy drinks at Happy Hour prices. Don't ask me how I know that.

View at Middleton Place 2018. There are alligators lurking. Believe it!
Photo by author.

CHAPTER 30

Garden Tours

NEVER CONFUSE A Charleston garden tour with a pub crawl. Many elements are similar, but the pub crawl will not be as likely to leave a hangover.

From time to time Charlestonians, as a welcoming gesture, open their homes and private gardens for tours. They do so with officious names like "Annual Festival of Homes," but we're really talking about the blooming gardens. These events are scheduled around the birds and the bees (pollination). Timing is everything.

What will a tourist experience? Fine wines are popular. If the husband is home, he's likely sipping a vodka tonic or a fine single-malt scotch over the rocks. Look for that guy. He'll pour one for you, too.

Often, these tours are done for a charitable entity. Sometimes a charity is the leading catalyst for success. An open bar helps. Ask the experts who organize fundraising auctions. Booze helps. Do you ever notice the wide-open cocktail hour before the bids start? It works.

The private gardens are a meticulous hobby of the many. The right amount of water, fertilizer, and sunshine are essential. Charlestonians are proud of their hydrangeas, wisteria, jasmine, tea olives, oleander, crepe myrtles, hyacinths, dogwoods, camellias, gardenias, and azaleas. The varieties dazzle the eye. The arrangement and bloom cycles are crafted for effect. Yards usually have water features—fountains, ponds, and bird baths.

Check out the shaded side yards with a Charleston staple—the joggling board. If it is not painted Charleston green (green so dark that it is black), the joggling board is not authentic. The hurricane shutters should sport the same color. Yes, hurricane shutters. We have earthquake rods, as well. The condition of disasters pending gives us another reason to offer visitors our rum drinks, whiskeys, and fine wines.

Do you need to buy a ticket for a garden tour? Well, yes. But if you missed it, don't fret. I had a friend that had an elegant garden in his backyard on Church Street. He said tourists often just walked into his backyard and took pictures. I asked if he objected to the invasion of privacy, but he just smiled. He said that he got used to it over the years and just greeted them as if he were the Chamber of Commerce. Then he told me that his easy-going neighbors got even more wanderer-visitors than he did. The lesson? Flaunt em if you got em.

Everybody enjoys a beautiful garden.

King Street, Charleston. Quaint and narrow, it
accepts thin bills in high denominations.
Photo by author.

W. THOMAS MCQUEENEY

CHAPTER 31

Museums the Way You See Ums

MANY YEARS AGO, a fine Charleston lady was elected to serve as president of the Confederate Museum on Meeting Street. The vestige organization had plenty of artifacts and space, but no money and no plan for survival other than by the physical effort. The museum was dilapidated.

The dedicated lady traveled to the museum each Monday afternoon when it was closed. She unlocked the door and then locked it on the inside. Her two young daughters accompanied her. She disrobed to her slip so that she could spend hours dusting and vacuuming the Market Hall tenancy. Her two daughters cleaned the windows and the glass tops to the display cases. Being the Charleston chapter 4 president of the United Daughters of the Confederacy was more duty than an honor. That fine Charleston lady was my grandmother.

The few tourists who passed through Charleston paid $2 each to tour the Civil War relics. The accumulation of funds could be used to make repairs—barely. The UDC had little money and scant income from visitors and memberships.

The building remains a sample of Greek Revival architecture that has withstood the calamities. Well, almost. It was a Shriners' meeting house in 1838 when it fell victim to the city's conflagration of that year (the Great Charleston Fire). That same conflagration devoured other important buildings including St. Mary's Church, a theater, and a newly built hotel. Even a steamboat in the harbor, the *Neptune*, caught fire.[71]

The museum had a boomerang background. It was rebuilt in 1841. Here, young men rushed into Charleston from all over the South to join the Confederate Army in 1861. They signed up at the Market Hall.[72] After a four-year war that devastated every faction of America, the forlorn soldiers returned. The UDC was founded in 1894 by ladies that felt that the valor of their husbands, brothers, and fathers should be celebrated despite the result. A war reunion took place in Charleston in 1899. Since the old soldiers were coming anyway, the UDC asked them to bring their old uniforms, their belts, and buttons, their caps, and gloves. They even landed a few swords. The collection became significant enough to merit a museum. The City of Charleston's council—all of whom were Confederate Veterans—allowed the UDC the space above the city market.[73] There isn't enough weaponry and swords to start another war, but there are plenty of interesting items.

In the 1788 land transfer agreement, Charles Cotesworth Pinckney ceded the market area to the city. The express usage was to remain a market in perpetuity with no human being ever to be sold on the donated land.[74] The Market was for wares, meat, fish, and poultry in addition to farm vegetables. Despite misinformed tour guide propaganda, there were no slaves sold at the market. The Market Hall is seen today as most living Charlestonians saw it many years ago. The paint and upkeep have been much better than my grandmother could have provided each Monday in her slip with her diligent daughters.

Several other old Charleston fixtures keep us immersed in the past.

The Gibbes Museum of Art was completely renovated in 2017. It is spectacular. The exhibits include artifacts out of the ordinary. It houses a collection of miniature portraits. They are large enough to view without artificial lenses. The Gibbes has much more—such as normal-sized art, sculpture, and heirloom photographs.

There is a Karpeles Manuscript Museum that was installed into an old uptown Methodist church on Spring Street. The church was devastated by Hurricane Hugo in 1989. The Karpeles group bought it and repaired yet another Greek Revival building.[75] One wonders why they have manuscripts instead of books. Karpeles has other museums in other cities that continually rotate exhibits. The exhibition of Samuel F. B. Morse coincided with this paragraph. But the paragraphs herein will also be rotated later by an editor I haven't met yet.

Charleston is building a magnificent black history museum near the South Carolina Aquarium. Early indications are that the museum will be the only one of its kind anywhere in the world. But then again, Charleston is the only city of its kind anywhere in the world. Charleston is the most appropriate place in America for the black history museum. Why? It's because more slaves from Africa and the West Indies were brought to North America through Charleston than any other place. It is an ignoble fact, but we mustn't shy away from what was wrong and dehumanizing. Museums help us to learn and respect others.

There is the Old Slave Mart Museum on Chalmers Street. It is quaint and has startling artifacts. Whatever you do, never go there in a car that has bad shock absorbers. You may end up in traction. Chalmers Street is paved with cobblestones.

Several years ago, my first cousin brought some really old stuff to my house. We sat and ruminated over what to do with the packed boxes. His mother (my aunt) passed away, and these boxes had some significant—but not valuable—old stuff. After we drank a few more ruminations, we decided to see if the Charleston Museum could use any of it. *Shonuff,* they took much of it. They cataloged my great grandfather's long underwear, my granny's diary from 1908, the daguerreotypes, and a few nineteenth-century household items. There was an ironing board that was just a rounded oak board that one could iron upon. It didn't come from Sears. There were journals from a doctor's office (the same great-grandfather who wore long underwear was a doctor). The pages showing services provided and charges validated the normal physicians' pricing structure from those times. Today's appendectomy charges would have paid my great grandfather ten years of income.

The Charleston Museum had a similar "returning Confederate soldier" history that was noted for the Market Hall. When they came back in 1899, an ugly large two-story building was constructed in just three months at the corner of Calhoun Street and Rutledge Avenue. But the veterans couldn't stay forever, so the big hairy building needed a new purpose. It became the Charleston Museum in 1907.[76] It smelled much like a musty old museum because that's what it was when I ran around in there in the 1950s. Because the building was massive, the exhibits were spread out. It became the city's attic.

Though there were items like mummies and Mastodon tusks, there were also odd things like the skeleton of a right whale that made a wrong turn and was hunted down mercilessly in Charleston Harbor. At first, some thought the whale to be the returning H. L. Hunley submarine—which had disappeared over thirty years earlier. To wit, the historic Hunley submarine was found in 1995 and raised in 2000, nearly 140 years after it went missing. While the actual Hunley submarine is being preserved in North Charleston, the replica built from specifications of the original sits in front of the new Charleston Museum. It looks nothing like a whale. The whale skeleton remains as the central attraction hung from the ceiling in the new museum on Meeting Street. The Charleston Museum organization is the oldest in the country (1773), but the building that houses it is relatively new.

It's hard to put old stuff in old buildings anymore. We Geechee Charlestonians like to put new stuff in old buildings and old stuff in new buildings. Somehow, that works out much better.

Charleston has a children's museum. It just doesn't seem like they are old enough to have their own museum, but they do. It is non-profit, much like my first few books, and accentuates the creative process for those little rascals pulling on you when you're in the other museums.

The College of Charleston houses the Mace Brown Museum of Natural History. They have fifteen thousand artifacts, and their displays of dinosaur skeletons were set up by the professors to scare the children in the aforementioned children's museum. The Citadel has a museum on campus, as well. It is on the third floor of the Daniel Library. I used the second floor of the library to sleep when I was a cadet there posing as a student. There are items related to The Citadel's founding and involvement in wars since 1846. The museum even has a hardtack biscuit that was served in the Mess Hall in 1858. There's a bite missing. It tastes the same as the new biscuits.

There are other places of interest that come under the "museum" heading. Patriot's Point is the entryway to the Vietnam Memorial village and to the Fighting Lady, the Yorktown aircraft carrier. That's a big museum! On the Yorktown, stroll through the Medal of Honor Museum. That museum will have its own building at Patriot's Point in a few years. They only need a hundred million dollars more than they have at this writing.

In Charleston, some very impressive antebellum and pre-Revolutionary homes are de facto museums. These are very much worth seeing—the Nathaniel Russell House, Heyward-Washington House, Calhoun Mansion, Joseph Manigault House, Aiken-Rhett House and the Edmondston-Alston House. People thrived in these homes. See how they flourished in the wealthiest city in America prior to the Civil War (or "that recent unpleasantness").

Charleston itself is the largest living museum in America. Unlike Williamsburg, Virginia (a fabulous site), Charleston is quite alive. The city now flaunts the architecture that we could not afford to tear down. It was a propitious conundrum. People come to see what two wars and a hundred-year economic disaster did not disturb. The welcome of the Geechees makes it that much better.

The city was built on the trade winds. The tall ships
from around the world come to the port often.
Photo by author.

CHAPTER 32

The Port of Charleston

IT'S LIKELY YOU have never heard of James Adger. By 1858 (the year of his death), he was considered among the wealthiest men in America. He was Bill Gates diversified. He had a steamship line, a factoring warehouse, and a mercantile hardware store. Most of his fortune was derived from his career as a merchant banker. He served in the U.S. House of Representatives.[77]

Adger was an Irishman from County Antrim who brought a stacked assemblage of the Giant's Causeway to Charleston, variously listed among the Eight Natural Wonders of the World. He had it installed on the Portico of Meeting Street's Hibernian Hall in 1851. The rest of the Giant's Causeway is still intact as basalt columns that step to the sea in Northern Ireland. They're over ten thousand years old. Go and see for yourself. Adger's gift to his Hibernian friends is still on the front portico of that 1841 building. He picked up many a bar tab there, so the prized column was gleefully received.

Because Charleston has a deep natural port, shipping was—and still is—a major economic contributor. Our cobblestone streets are a testament to world-class shipping trade. As you know by now, cobblestones are not native to the area. They are ship's ballasts that came from European ports.

Sailing ships found a river in the ocean. The Gulf Stream augmented the journey as ships from the Atlantic European ports and on into the Mediterranean Sea followed the wind in its clockwise circle to the West Indies and up the American east coast. The major Southern port of Charleston brought wares to include spices, tea, refined clothing, and crafted furnishings. Sailing vessels left with several regional commodities, most notably cotton, tobacco, and rice. Many patrons of world trade besides James Adger became wealthy. They were in Charleston, too.

The sailing ships were tall enough to see on the horizon easily, so they called them "tall ships." There were frigates, schooners, barks, clippers, cutters, corvettes, brigantines, and caravels. Anyone who knew the differences could move to the high battery and be the head spotter of ships. All of the mercantile ships had much in common. They needed stuff when they got to Charleston. The ships needed rope, candlewax, tar, canvas, or oaken repairs. The folks that sailed them ashore required other commodities like port wine, rum, beer, food, and women. Their checklists were not in that particular order.

The simple sense of anticipating needs was a business best suited for Charleston entrepreneurs. The houses on East Battery lined up to welcome the tall ships. Many of these were built upon the benefits of port trade. And there were other houses on back alleys that helped the sailors spend their shore leave shillings. But this book is for general audiences.

The entrepreneur Robert William Roper's house was built in 1838. He was a wealthy cotton plantation owner who knew they would come to get his cotton. His neighbor, John Ravenel at 5 East Battery, was the president of the South Carolina Railroad. He knew that tall ships meant more income incoming, as well.

The house down the street built by a shipping merchant, Charles Edmondston (from the Shetland Islands) turned a few heads. Edmondston waited for the Battery seawall to be established before he built the mansion. Nobody likes the harbor in their yard on full moon tides.

Those three homes are iconic to the first view of Charleston from the water. They have iconic values, as well. Recently a tour guide friend told me that no home in the first two blocks of East Battery is worth less than $7 million. I guess I will not be watching as my ship comes in.

Have I mentioned the South Carolina State Ports Authority yet? The SCSPA is the real mover and shaker in Charleston. They were developed because shipping took a left turn while heading north. The deep and wide harbor made it so.

Though the State Ports Authority was not officially chartered until 1942, the state was already here, and the port was, too. Authority was a given motivation.

Shipping has been going on in our harbor since 1670. Though other significant ports are dotting the map, Charleston is the real deal. The prevailing cargo is of the containership variety in colorful metal boxes that can be easily converted to over-the-road trucking passage. There are also car carriers—large car-carrying ships that load in Charleston. There used to be banana boats from Cuba that came in regularly, but a little missile crisis changed all of that back in 1962.

Each day, six container ships leave Charleston harbor with loads valued at $150,000,000 or more. But don't sit at the pier and watch them. You'll suffer an awful sunburn.

Cruise ships have found us. If you ever want to get a downtown Charleston homeowner talking a bit louder, ask him or her what they think about the beautiful cruise ships that dock up at the passenger terminal. Then step back.

Up until 1996, we had a U.S. Naval Base and naval shipyard repair facility—for U.S. Navy Ships. We had really cool submarines here, too. They were neat to see traveling under the big bridges when the sailors returned from world cruises.

My navy veteran father would have been the worst submariner ever. He was too tall at six feet, three inches, and he was claustrophobic. Yet he and my mother crammed a hungry baseball team into a four-room rental house during my formative years. To be clear, I wouldn't have traded that experience for a $7 million home on the High Battery.

It was with mixed emotions for the entire community when the U. S. Navy with the submarines left us. But still to this day, by tradition, young dating couples park at the High Battery late on Friday evenings to watch the Charleston Harbor Submarine Races. I've been there; done that.

Our deepwater port is why The Adventure arrived here in 1670. It is why we benefit as the major Atlantic shipping port in the southeast.

REMEMBRANCES OF THINGS PAST

Carriage tours take visitors to the history.
Photo by author.

CHAPTER 33

Here Hugo

INITIALLY, THEY SAID it would not hit Charleston. They were my neighbors who had just planted new shrubbery and put up a backyard fence made of brick. He was a CPA. She was a schoolteacher. The weather people were a bit more technical. They said that a monster storm was moving west-north-west. That was not good. Hurricane Hugo was east-south-east of Charleston. I made my hotel reservation in North Charleston. Surely, it would not reach me way up there!

When that monster hurricane was barreling across the Atlantic, our mayor with the most admirable Geechee nomenclature called it something else. To the world, they are hurry-canes, but to Charlestonians, they were herakins.

I've often wondered why the names of hurricanes do not include the holy family. There's been no Hurricane Jesus or Mary or Joseph. They've skipped other biblical names like Moses, Jeremiah, Enoch, and Malachi. There are no satanic names either like Beelzebub and Lucifer. My guess is that the naming gurus do not want to associate weather disasters with good and evil.

The slightly odd names show up in hurricanes. In order, we had three to hit Charleston named Hugo, Floyd, and Gaston. Gaston is a French medieval name that means "strange guest." They got that one right.

When Hurricane Hugo hit in September of 1989, the local county council chairperson sent out a terse message to those fools thinking about staying. The message was, "If you can hear my voice, get out!" What kind of idiot wouldn't heed that ominous warning? I pondered that question fully as I stared out of the window at the North Charleston Sheraton to see a small pickup truck blown across the parking lot. That was at 9:00 p.m. The hurricane's calm eye didn't pass through until midnight. I know that because I went out the rear of the hotel to experience being in the eye of a hurricane. Check that one off the bucket list. I'll never do it again.

By 9:30 p.m. on that harrowing evening, electrical transformers were blowing out in clouds of blue sparks across the horizon. By 10:15 p.m., the hotel manager came to every door to tell the occupants to get out of the rooms because of glass breakage. My $139 room included breakfast and a comfy bed. Instead, I laid down with a pillow in a hallway and listened to the loudest sustained sounds I had ever heard. Fortunately, I sat next to the CNN news crew from Atlanta. They knew when to go out into the eyewall. I did just that. It was eerily weird and weirdly eerie at the same time—calmness near midnight in a parking lot of destruction.

At 5:30 a.m. I arose from my hallway sleeping spot and went down for the free breakfast. They still owe me. With no electricity, no food, no employees, and nobody else there, I felt like I drifted into a bit part of an apocalyptic movie.

Luckily, I had parked my car safely where the hotel blocked the wind. It had been pelted by the small pebbles blown from the hotel's flat roof. The paint job looked like a giant tin face of horrible acne. But it started up. The windshield was not cracked! I then went to see if my home was still in the same county.

As I left the hotel parking area, no street lighting or traffic signals were working. Getting around the random debris was a challenge. My office was near. All of the signage was down. As I entered Interstate 26, I found that I was the only vehicle on the road. It was Twilight Zone 1989. Soon I caught up with a caravan of trucks from Florida Power and Light. They had to leave pretty early to be getting there at that hour.

Getting to my neighborhood was easy, but getting into my neighborhood was nearly impossible. Something on the order of five hundred pine trees had fallen like the scene from a nuclear explosion. I parked my car near the highway and began jumping over and going around trees to make my way back a few blocks to my home. My wife and children had traveled to a safe inland home. Only a fool would stay.

It was nearly 6:15 a.m. There was no one else around. Even the squirrels were stunned. Once I reached my house, I was elated to see it still standing and only a few pine trees leaning on the roof. There was other damage to the front, side, and rear. The backyard was another

Sullivans Island lighthouse has seen many ships but
has never spotted the wind! Photo by author.

story—more pines and gum trees down. Our fencing and decking was destroyed. Being in the insurance industry, I realized that I would have a long day. I checked the inside of my home and moved a limb from a window. I taped the opening, then left to check on my office interior.

When my insurance agency sold all of those home, auto, and boat policies, I had not expected to have twenty-nine hundred claims to necessitate coverage all at once. I knew other long-term agents that had twice as many. An agent friend in Summerville had sixty-three hundred. Preparing my office for a day's deluge was the priority. Without electricity, the office was dark inside. There was an inch of water on the floor from the failed roof system. I moved folding tables to the parking lot. There were no computers. We could only record claims by an improvised system. A yellow pad with a name, an address, a severity code from 1 to 5 was utilized. We added a phone number in anticipation that phone service could be soon restored. There were no cell phones then.

I figured that people might show up in a demanding mob. They didn't.

Most sane Charlestonians were still out of town. Yet many still experienced the storm. Hugo was still a category 1 hurricane when it hit Charlotte, North Carolina. That's two hundred miles inland! Hurricane Hugo was the most massive recorded storm ever to hit the United States. No wonder that pickup truck was blown across the parking lot!

The Friday morning after the storm had very few claimants.

As the sun went down on September 22, I was exhausted from the lack of sleep the prior evening and went home to crawl over the pines to my bedroom. But someone told me to stop by the Piggly Wiggly parking lot on Highway 7 because the store manager was grilling steaks. It was true. He had side salads, dinner rolls, and green beans, too. He had set up a new grill with charcoal and began cooking steaks free for everyone who came. He had sweet tea without ice, paper plates, plastic dinnerware, and napkins. His cold storage system was not likely to operate anytime soon, so he said he'd rather feed the storm survivors than throw away product. What a patriot! I slept that evening after enjoying a hot meal with people I hardly knew. The Piggly Wiggly store manager incident was one of the dozens of stories that gave me great faith in the kindness of others in the face of adversity.

My agency office opened Saturday and Sunday and worked through the next three weekends taking claims without the benefit of electricity, phone service, ice, or pizza delivery. In all, we worked twenty-eight straight days from first light to dark without a day off. My staff was incredible. Many others, including family, came to help. A former employee who had taken another job came because her office was destroyed, and she wanted to pitch in. My retired father came in to help. He stayed and retired again ten years later!

Six months later, Charleston was still cleaning up from Hurricane Hugo.

From the experience, I gained several warm observations:

1. Charlestonians were civil and helped one another. A World War II veteran who landed at Normandy came by one day to see if he could provide lunch for my staff. A former employee, Suzanne, showed up and asked if she could volunteer for a few weeks. Her CPA firm was closed. She later became the CFO for a major corporation. It was likely because of her kindness and professionalism. My sister Sharon delivered ice and water to us from Charlotte. My brother Ritchie did the same from Columbia. Others pitched in. At the end, the scorecard read 2900 claims with no lawsuits. Now that's an achievement!

2. There were new roofs everywhere. Roofers came in from Arkansas and Iowa. Every Charleston home, it seemed, installed a new roof. The local roofing companies lost the repair market for a decade.

3. Churches and charitable organizations were conduits for goodness. However, some insensitive entrepreneurs drove from other states in U-Haul trucks with generators, ice coolers, gas cans, batteries, and chainsaws that they would sell on-the-spot for triple the retail price. Most folks were disgusted by these price-gouging schemes, but these opportunists probably sold out anyway.

4. There was little or no looting. There were few reports of crime.

5. People brought in bottled water from everywhere. Everybody's water was contaminated—mostly by pinesap seepage into the water supply. We could only drink the bottled water. Everyone's shower and bath experience left that person smelling like

Pine-Sol cleaner. I told everyone that my aftershave lotion was a new brand, Scent of Windblown Pine.

6. Phone service was restored within ten days for most. When my office got phone service back, very busy grew into ridiculously busy.

7. The sounds of Charleston from early morning to late at night were that of portable gas generators and constant chainsaws. We got used to it. We were on the road to normalcy.

8. When television and radio service returned, the faces of the reporters changed. They were champs! It was fashionable not to look fresh for a few weeks. The male announcers showed razor stubble and open-collared shirts instead of the usual make-up and Armani suits. Some of the women reporters were beginning to look like the men.

9. You could hear my whole neighborhood cheer in joy three weeks later—when the electricity grid was restored.

10. The mayors, the fire departments, the police, the businesses, and the hospitals were particularly effective and tireless. Together they turned a disaster into a heart-warming story of perseverance.

Oh yeah, my neighbors lost their shrubbery and their new brick fence. We laughed about their week-old brick fence years later. It was rubble.

My best Hurricane Hugo claims' story was about a powerful and honest man, named JJ. JJ was a Geechee to the tenth power. After Hurricane Hugo, there was scant uncontracted labor to remove trees and branches from homes. A homeowner could perform the work, or wait until a crew might come weeks later. Everyone willing to do so worked chainsaws. Even my mother operated a chainsaw. Come to think of it, I did too.

When some claimants came into my insurance office for advice and assistance, many questions were asked. JJ came in one day and asked me if we had a program to pay the homeowner to remove their own trees. We did. Back then, we paid $10 per hour to remove one's own debris. I told JJ to keep a reasonable record of hours for the work and bring it in when he finished. I would write a check to him the day he finished. JJ had eleven pine trees leaning on his home near Ladson, South Carolina.

JJ came in a week later with a yellow tablet sheet listing his hours. He worked fifty-four of them. I was momentarily stunned at the number but did as promised and paid JJ $540 on a claim draft. I knew that the number was an honest accounting because I knew JJ. But out of curiosity, I had to ask.

"JJ, did you keep running out of gas for the chainsaw. Is that why it took so long?" I asked.

He answered in his Geechee best, "Chainsaw? What chainsaw? I ain't had no chainsaw, man! I used dee ax," he informed. "I wush we ada chainsaw. T'woulda been easier, fo sho."

"With $540, you can buy one now, that is, if there are any to be bought," I said. "Wow, JJ. I'm impressed that it didn't take you even more time."

JJ was a fit and muscular six-foot, four-inch man with a great smile. I was wholly impressed by his diligence and energy.

He said sincerely, "Mr. Tommy, I did my neighbor's hoose too cuz he ain't had no surance. But dat wuz a gift."

JJ was the man! As he left, someone else in my office that overheard the conversation commented, "Aren't you glad that JJ didn't take those trees down with a pocketknife?"

Hurricane Hugo was the major natural disaster of my lifetime. But my memory of it is profound. It made all of us better people.

The Citadel was founded in 1842. The campus
is open to the public. Photo by author

W. THOMAS MCQUEENEY

CHAPTER 34

Charleston's Most Underrated Attractions

THERE IS SO much to see in Charleston that the pace could be dizzying. Relax. I've got you covered. There are some attractions you shouldn't miss that are either free or close to free. They'll have you leaving here much more informed and satisfied.

Getting to the Angel Oak is easy. Take Maybank Highway until it hits Bohicket Road. You're there. Well placed signs will take you the other half-block of travel. It's an amazing site and you just wouldn't believe an oak tree could be that big, that old, and that beautiful. It's the kind of awe you may have enjoyed when first seeing the Grand Canyon. But it won't take anything near the travel effort, it's free, and you'll have time to see much, much more. Don't get lost and end up at the Grand Canyon.

With bias, the one place that is most accessible and bargain-priced for a full day of interactive activities has to be the USS Yorktown aircraft carrier. Your kids will love it. The views are spectacular. Check out the Laffey and the sound effects of the Vietnam village, too. You could spend hours in their gift shop afterward.

Speaking of unique gift shops, check out the Historic Charleston Foundation Gift Shop on Meeting Street across from Hibernian Hall. Be ready to be blown away by their Charleston-themed array of local cookies, books, ties, benches, and candles. If this book is not displayed there, complain to management!

Do you like to sit in the shade? Try Washington Park. The statuary, busts, and obelisk come with the attachment of history. It's idyllic. While there, you might saunter on over to the Fireproof Building (built without flammables in 1827). The Fireproof Building is what it's named. The South Carolina Historical Society holds many historical documents there. It's free.

The Waring Library (175 Ashley Avenue) is in a gorgeous setting just down from where I grew up. My family contributed many medical artifacts. It displays a history of the health sciences. It's free, but you have to make an appointment. Tell them I said you're okay. This book is your ticket.

Did you know that the only operating tea plantation in the United States is just out from downtown a way? If you're already at the Angel Oak, go back to Maybank Highway and turn left. The tea plantation is about ten more miles out on Wadmalaw Island. It's free, too! There is a minimal charge for the trolley tour. It has a nice gift shop. You can guess what they sell.

Another gorgeous free site is Mepkin Abbey near Moncks Corner. It is run by the Trappist Order (and silence is in order). It's another freebie. Walk in reverence.

One of former Mayor Joe Riley's visionary upgrades is the Riley Waterfront Park. He didn't name it that. The city council did after he retired. It has a terrific view of the harbor where we send out regattas full of sailboats for your enhanced Charleston entertainment. There are shady oaks, a large concrete wharf with swings, a fabulous jump-on-in fountain and plenty of benches. The price is free and so is the laughter of the children.

Every Friday afternoon at 3:30 when The Citadel is in session, there is a military parade on campus. Be there by 3:15 for a seat. It lasts an hour. Two thousand cadets in uniform is impressive. The Regimental Band and the cannon fire make it special. Oh yeah. It's free.

If you haven't taken in the Visitors Center train station reproduction on Meeting Street yet, why are you waiting? It gives you a plethora of ideas for your visit and it's cozy and comfortable. They can tell you about many discounts. They can get your trolley passes. There's even a brilliant short movie to entice you for your stay.

That museum just across the street from the Visitors Center has my great-grandfather's 1890s underwear. Don't tell my great-grandmother. The Charleston Museum is worth triple the admission price.

My favorite thing to do in Charleston is to have no agenda and just walk around. And I'm a Geechee local. I'm still amazed at what was and what now is. If you see me just suggest that I should get home by dark.

Strategically, Fort Sumter protected Charleston harbor. But its ramifications changed a nation. Photo by author.

CHAPTER 35

Charleston's Art Renaissance

T HOSE THAT ENJOY the exquisite visual arts at the Annual Southeastern Wildlife Exposition in Charleston are routinely impressed by the volume and quality of art talent it represents. There is nothing like it. Charleston and the art world have had a long and happy marriage. We even had our own Renaissance!

There were those art aficionados with passions and predispositions for everything Charleston that left us in bygone years. They were our grandmothers, our family doctors, and our ninth-grade history teachers. A bygone era of instructive bygone heroes they were. One would have believed that art never took a holiday from the Holy City. But it did.

The War between the States took away the time and resources for such dalliances as the visual arts. It took six decades before a remarkable period of Charleston history heralded its return.

Born in 1883, Elizabeth O'Neill Verner became the focal artist of an entire cultural movement that placed Charleston scenes above the mantles of visitors from Boston to Baton Rouge. To be sure, there were others—much akin to the Parisian entourage of writer's and artists of the 1920's and 1930's (Ernest Hemingway, Pablo Picasso, F. Scott Fitzgerald, Gertrude Stein, Henri Matisse). In Charleston, a visitor could enjoy Verner, along with Alice Ravenel Huger Smith (1876–1958), and DuBose Heyward (1885–1940). Others arrived from elsewhere.

"Come quickly, have found heaven." This was the telegram sentiment of Alfred Hutty[78] (1877-1954), a Michigander artist who sent it to his wife. Hutty had recently arrived in the place Verner had always called home—but he was on his way to Florida! Others, like Anna Heyward Taylor (1879-1956) traveled the world. Like Verner, this South Carolinian was part of the crested wave that became the Charleston Art Renaissance.

James Sauls wrote in Art and Artists of the South,

Probably the best-known twentieth-century woman artist of Charleston was Elizabeth O'Neill Verner. The daughter of a rice-broker, she received her early education in Charleston and Columbia, South Carolina. Her artistic ability already apparent at the age of fourteen (the year she sold her first painting), she received encouragement from Alice Ravenel Huger Smith, the Charleston artist. Verner enrolled at the Pennsylvania Academy of the Fine Arts in 1903, studying for two years before returning to Charleston. Soon after her return, she married E. Pettigrew Verner and raised a family of two children while painting scenes of Charleston in her spare time. In 1923, shortly after completing her first etching, she helped to organize the Charleston Society of Etchers. When her husband died in 1925, Verner turned to her art as a means of supporting herself and her family and became a prolific pastellist and printmaker.[79]

She was looked upon as Charleston's art celebrity. My mother (Charlotte Simmons McQueeney), one of the eleven local artists who formed the Charleston Artists Guild in 1953, took lessons from Elizabeth O'Neill Verner.

No one artist had the range of impact as did Verner. She had an array of talent. Her passion for etching moved her to the forefront of the known technology. Anybody can learn to etch, but Verner used it as the most potent reproduction medium of her time. Her exquisite etchings are now the pride of the most informed collectors. Verner filled her palette with the colors of the Lowcountry. She examined the times past with oil reminiscences of outlying plantations, shrimping boats, and those dedicated souls that weaved sweetgrass baskets on the city market. Verner created a style in her pastels of the dominant church spires and the old dusky mansions. She drew people in their vignettes, from the walk of Broad Street to the dockworkers.

Verner opened a gallery to sell her art in 1924. She was far ahead of her time.

She wrote about her experiences. Verner published five books. A passage from her 1941 book, Mellowed by Time, gives insight to her pride of the community:

"… I feel it when I glide in through the narrow channel at the jetties and see across the harbor the skyline of the city with the gleam of St. Philip's cross, St. Michael's white spire, the copper domes of the old Scotch Church and far uptown the slender steeple of St. Matthew's, still our skyscrapers. What a world of heroism that narrow channel has witnessed, so close Ft. Moultrie on one side and Fort Sumter on the other, and yet between these two a gap was once so wide that it split a nation. Such a very small city it is, compared to most cities, so confined by its rivers and harbor that it has been compressed and become an essence of itself. It is impossible for me to enter Charleston from any side, whether by land or sea and not feel that here the land is precious; here is a place worth keeping; this, of all the world, is home."

Her insights were borne in prose. Verner's lasting significance to the genre, you ask? The South Carolina Arts Commission established a statewide award in 1972. The award, a bronze statue given to symbolize excellence is named for Elizabeth O'Neill Verner.

They describe it accordingly:

> Elizabeth O'Neill Verner achieved an international reputation for her etchings and pastels, many of which capture the spirit of the South Carolina Lowcountry. She was also a teacher, writer, and historian. Throughout her 96 years, Mrs. Verner traveled abroad extensively. Drawings of South Carolina residences, churches, and street-life portraits are Verner trademarks recognized throughout the world for the way they capture South Carolina's unique people and architecture.[80]

The old buildings she committed to canvas are still visually dynamic. The plantation houses are, if anything, even more beautiful. Verner and her contemporaries brought Charleston to the world. She was the "Belle of the Charleston Renaissance."

An 1881 visit from the Irish author and playwright Oscar Wilde best illustrated the mood of the times before the Renaissance. His visit was recorded by the media.

When asked about the advancement of the arts in Charleston, Wilde replied,

> "I like the Southern people, although you have let the Northern people get ahead of you in art. I think you are more adapted to the cultivation of art, I mean the decorative art. You are of a warmer temperament and of a more imaginative turn of mind, don't you know. I

should think you would turn your attention more to art. You have magnificent forests, beautiful flowers. What you want is more diversity."[81]

It took forty years for Wilde's observances to surface in the Holy City's surge of creativity. It spurred the future. Today, the Spoleto Arts Festival is the largest of its kind in the United States.

In the modern Charleston, one would be challenged to walk three blocks in the commercial and business areas of the city without encountering an exquisite art gallery. Charleston became a magnificent city of the arts—but there was a period when art took a long nap. Elizabeth O'Neill Verner woke us up.

Cathedral of St. John the Baptist on watercolor circa 1960.
By Charlotte Simmons McQueeney

CHAPTER 36

Religious Fervor

MANY THINK WE are called The Holy City because of the overabundance of churches across our peninsula—nearly two hundred! But that's the result, not the reason. The right of religious freedom earned us the moniker.

Religious freedom. Both ideological zealots and dictatorial governments from much of the world are still withholding it. It seems simple that we should leave people alone and let them pray or not pray in the manner that they interpret their personal beliefs.

The major religions certainly have a stake in the ideal of freedom. They can market their faith or witness it accordingly. Tent revivals and celebratory holidays (which are "holy-days") can gather the flock. We Geechees got that religious freedom deal right. The deep port brought many who had been persecuted intensely. To be sure, our 1670 marketing department made a big splash. After wading through the first ninety-six articles of the Fundamental Constitutions of Carolina, the author-philosopher John Locke did well with Article 97:

> "...the natives who...are utterly strangers to <u>Christianity</u>, whose <u>idolatry</u>, ignorance, or mistake gives us no right to expel or use them ill; and those who remove from other parts to plant there will unavoidably be of different opinions concerning matters of religion, the <u>liberty</u> whereof they will expect to have allowed them...and also that <u>Jews</u>, <u>heathens</u>, and other dissenters from the purity of <u>Christian</u> religion may not be scared and kept at a distance from it...therefore, any seven or more persons agreeing in any religion, shall constitute a church or profession, to which they shall give some name, to distinguish it from others."[82]

It's a wrap.

We guaranteed the rights of all who came and all who were already here, including the cannibalistic Westo Indians. Article 97 is why the Jewish faith was welcomed and grew in Charleston and had no fear of the latent craziness—like the Spanish Inquisition established in 1478 to detect heretics. Of all the Spanish calamities (the Spanish Civil War, the Spanish Flu, the loss of the Spanish Armada, Spanish-American War, Spanish-Catalonian Divide), the Spanish Inquisition remains the worst. The Spanish did not come to Charleston.

The Quakers came, as did the Methodists and the Lutherans. Surely we had Circs. Circs? It's a local term for worshipper in our Circular Congregational Church. Check it out. The church is an architectural outlier. Its walls are circular. Even its pews are circular!

But I should circle back.

Things that happened around the world had an impact upon what was a growing population in Charleston. When King Louis XIV revoked the 1598 Edict of Nantes[83] in 1685, our little colony was barely a teenager. The reversal sent the French Huguenots fleeing to other places. Charleston had some openings. Thus, we have the country's only French Huguenot church.

When the Haitian Revolution began in 1791, the French Catholics needed a new port. They had just established the first Catholic Church in the Carolinas and Georgia (St. Mary's on Hasell Street, pronounced as "Hazel"). At that time the congregation was mostly Irish. The graveyard markers show the French influence.

The Baptist religion emanated from Maine, but the *grits division* of the Southern Baptist Convention and Association was a movement that started in the Holy City in 1751.[84] Where Else? The faith strengthened here and spread across the southeast in a fervor.

The Scots had a great way to build their pedigree. They named their first Presbyterian Church in Charleston the First Scots Church. It worked! They even had a Second Scots Presbyterian Church. Chronology is alive and well in Presbyterian circles.

It can be said that the original church of the first settlers is Anglican. After the Revolution, the term became synonymous with Episcopal since Anglican referenced "English." The English had been expelled by December 1782. In recent years, because of severe divides in the Episcopal Church, the Anglican Church has resurfaced in Charleston.

The LDS Church has established identity into the Holy City. LDS is not "Lowcountry Designated Spirituals." It's Latter Day Saints. I might have joined the LDS a hundred years ago if they still had polygamy. Give me a half-dozen wives, and I'll get real rewards from my credit card mileage plan. The Mormon Church is everywhere, and they seem to have a fine and admirable sense of clean living.

We've tripped upon a nuance in religion, especially here in Geechee-Land. Some would say that the previously un-churched are recently re-churched as Evangelicals. A local Mount Pleasant Evangelical church, Seacoast, has grown to fourteen thousand regular Sunday attendees.[85] They went from zero to "wow!" in just thirty years (founded 1988). The most substantial membership growth in the Charleston Religious pie chart is the Evangelicals.

There are significant others—Greek Orthodox, African Methodist Episcopal, Seventh Day Adventists, and Pentecostals. There are very few Muslims here, but they do exist. There are even Mennonites. When we said, "Come one, come all," we accepted everyone.

Our largest group of those adhering to the ideal of freedom of religion is evident by their lack of being evident. The atheists, agnostics, and unaffiliated non-attenders (believers who stay home) make up nearly forty-three percent of our population. By law, they have a right to be or not be of whatever spiritual disposition they prefer or don't. That said, I'm a churchgoer because I like my faith and like the people I see on Sundays who also like the same faith. But I do not judge others or look for reasons to dislike other's faiths. In fact, sometimes I visit their churches and synagogues. Why not? It's a journey through both spirituality and history.

The Holy City has a chance to be much holier if we continue to keep an open mind.

In perspective, the Treaty of Nantes and the retreat of that treaty made Charleston a destination city 350 years ago. But that destination status has changed from religious freedom reasons to tourist preference reasons. Geechees like both.

Charleston Flower Lady circa 1954.
Watercolor by Charlotte Simmons McQueeney.

CHAPTER 37

Contributions of Culture Understood

THOUGH IT MAY seem that way, not all history began in Charleston. Geechee was not the world's first spoken language. The research shows other forces at work that happened in anticipation of Charleston.

Before we Geechees evolved and brought Charleston to the world stage, there were sundry other contributors. Grab a cold glass of sweet tea and let's walk through this together.

The well of life, archeologists say, sprang forth out of Africa. It's where hunter-gatherers are, as yet, hunting and gathering.

In a sense, we are all African-Americans—and African-Europeans—and African-Asians. The sub-Saharan culture brought much more to civilization's front porch like farming and governing leadership, not to mention the domestication of animals. Pity the tribesman that penned in the first hyena or lion. The early tribes also had the benefit of metallurgy for tools and the wheel for transport.

As advanced as the later civilizations of the Incas, Aztecs, and Mayans became in the Western Hemisphere, especially in the science of astronomy, they did not have the African enhancements. There was no wheel for transport, no metal tools or metal weapons—and very few domesticated animals. Incas you're confused, Aztec-nological as they were, they lowered Mayan your expectations!

The Africans dispersed in directions further south and east, and presumably north into Egypt, Persia, Greece, and India. China, Iberia, and Rome emerged. Tribal communities extended to Mongolia, Korea, Japan, and Scandinavia. Most of these civilizations evolved with little outside contact. I wasn't there, so I do not remember it. But I studied it enough to make sense of our Charleston.

All cultures added to advancements of society so that the Holy City could become a happy beneficiary.

The Chinese made gunpowder, paper, and spaghetti. They also gave us the compass. We had no idea where we were going until that directional moment.

The Persians were popular as tradesmen who interacted with the Chinese, Indians, and East Africans. They invented bricks, wine, tar, and the windmill. They also invented cookies, ice cream, and, ahem! taxes. Republicans insist that the early Persians must have been Democrats.

The people of India were inventive as well. They must have noticed seasonal clothing needs. They brought civilization cashmere wool (Kashmir), cotton clothing, and the buttons to keep dungarees up (from the port town of Dhunga). They refined sugar, developed cataract surgery, and unfortunately advanced a frustrating game called Pachisi (Parcheesi). My fiancée once hit me over the head with a game board when I rolled the perfect numbers to block her entrance. I was dumbfounded before I was founded dumb.

The Chinese, we're told, invented formal marriage. I blame them. They abhor Pachisi.

In the event that all of this is Greek to anyone, then let's proceed to that Hellenistic culture to find democracy, important architectural advancements, and the idea of "trial by jury." The Greeks built outdoor theaters for their comedies and tragedies—never to be confused with the quietness that follows a misunderstood punch line. Greek mythology is mythical. There were myths lying around everywhere before the Greeks claimed them as their own. The Greeks were myth-understood.

The Babylonians, the Chinese, and the Romans laid claim to the invention of the umbrella. It's simple to resolve. We just have to calculate where rain was first discovered. But give the Romans credit. They depended upon the gravity of water to keep their aqueducts from looking like pointless archways. Archways are never pointed. Romans made paved roads to Roman coliseums and Roman baths. And Romans were the first to wear socks. Their Etruscan socks were rarely color-coordinated with their Florentine togas.

The Scandinavians were fierce fighters and energetic travelers and tradesmen. They brought both the common safety match and dynamite to the world. The fuse came from elsewhere. They made zippers and paper clips, too. One wonders what prompted the invention of the thermometer? Just how cold was it? Ask Anders Celsius.

The Egyptians fascinate us. Those large toothy grins came from their use of toothbrushes and toothpaste. They also came up with high heels, ladies. So, blame the society of the pyramids. It was brilliant that they invented locks and keys at the same time. Otherwise, we would be left with millions of keys that go to nothing. They also came up with wigs. Come to think of it, I have never met a bald Egyptian.

The French invented braille, the bicycle, the pencil, and the electric iron. The Spanish invented the mop. Well, they also founded the beret, the cigarette, and the misnamed Molotov cocktail. That paints an interesting mental picture.

The Mongols, the Jews, and the Germanic tribes all had a hand in bringing civilization forward with invention. Try barbecue, bagels, and beer.

We should toast the Mesopotamians. They invented the wheel and then the chariot. They built the first plow and knew when to plant because they were the first astronomers and planned around the seasons. They were the first to write stuff down, to irrigate fields, and to utilize sanitation. They invented glassware. They were the first to attach a sail to a boat. They came up with support columns and the dome. Yet we cannot thank them. The Hittites conquered the last of the Mesopotamians. That's an appropriate name for those in hand-to-hand combat. But the Hittites had metal weapons. The Mesopotamians, in their zeal to make the world a better place, had no knives, swords, spears, or arrows. It was a fatal oversight.

The favorite cultural invention of our generation may well be the way in which we understand other cultures faster than one can read the tales of Marco Polo. It is the favorite tool of the uninformed that wants to be the ultra-informed. We call it the Internet. It's better than tar, toothpaste, and Pachisi combined. And so far, it's free. And without it, this information would have taken a year to gather![86]

Geechees invented hospitality. There were upstarts elsewhere before us, like the Trojans who built a deception of hospitality and a large wooden horse. It took many years to undo false welcoming. The Geechees did that.

Corner grocers were established by the Charleston Greek community.
This one is near the College of Charleston on Beaufain Street.
Photo by author.

CHAPTER 38

Greek Heritage from Gyros to Ouzo

WHERE DID ALL of the Charleston Greek Revival buildings come from? They're everywhere. They survived earthquakes in Greece and the Great Quake of 1886 in Charleston. Charleston has more than 2,800 buildings listed as national historic landmarks.[87] The Bethel Methodist Church, Hibernian Society Hall, and the City Market Hall are outstanding examples of Greek Revival architecture. There are more. It seems that Greeks built structures to last. The Parthenon has done quite well!

Just a few millennia after the Trojan Wars, the runner Phidippides first conquest of the marathon, the Parthenon's last stone emplacement, and Alexander the Great's early death, Charleston became a destination city. Yeah, it took a while.

Charleston became a destination for the Greek immigrants—more than most knew. The great promise of the American democracy was at one time, the great Greek invention of democracy. Thank you, Cleisthenes. He thrived as the leading vote-getter from about 500 BC. Cleisthenes had never imagined the Holy City or even the Cooper River Bridge Run.

Historically, Greece was comprised of city-states so the monolithic idea of a united Greece could confuse a modern mindset upon a map. There were Spartans, Athenians, Trojans, and Macedonians. Think Corinth, Thebes, and the Island of Rhodes.

In the year 2000, I traveled to Greece and found the scenery to be amazing. Why would anyone ever leave? However, with their deep economic struggles, one may assume our Hellenic friends may be at the precipice of other migrations. Charleston certainly benefitted from the influx of past Greek citizens departing for a new life. For the record, I have no Greek heritage—just a profound appreciation of that particular culture because of what it brought to the world, and to Charleston.

Cephalonia is a picturesque island that sent us our first Charleston contingent. One might find the legend of Homer's storybook king, Odysseus, there. Lord Byron explored it on one of his many literary journeys. [88] Its natural setting features rabbits, goats, and roaming wild horses. Despite this Utopian setting, many left to find a new beginning in America. They initially established a community in New Smyrna Beach, Florida. But when a treaty temporarily returned Florida to Spain in 1783, many migrated to Charleston. That was our gain. Pass the ouzo, please.

The Greeks had the pedigree of greatness. We all know of Plato, Socrates, and Aristotle. But do we recall that modern medicine has the foundation of the Hippocratic oath—essentially advising the doctors to "do no harm?" I wish that included the after-surgery medical bill. Hippocrates was no hypocrite.

Greeks covered it all. How about the maker of laws from Athens, Solon? Laws are good to have! Geechees follow most of them.

Who was that guy who gave us so much early history in the narrative form—Herodotus? Yep, that's the guy.

They say that all of Western philosophy started with Thales.[89] Geechee Philosophy 101 started with Thales-on-the-Creek and a case of beer.

Have you ever heard of the Archimedes principle? He was the greatest of the early mathematicians. We know that Archimedes had his principles, but Pythagoras had his own theorem.

Homer was a grand-slam poet, and nobody had reached the pinnacle of power by age thirty-two like Alexander the Great. He was only Alexander the baby as a newborn.

Other legendary leaders, like Pericles and Leonidas, preceded him. That Greek sense of contribution to humanity landed in Charleston. The significance of the wave that arrived in the late 1800s and early 1900s is that they stayed, pursued a greater life for their children, and flourished. The adage that an early Greek testimony to life was the question of a person's summary at death. Though no historian can confirm the adage of "Did he live with passion?" as the testament of a Greek funeral, it is a compelling sentiment. If it's not true, it should be.

Growing up here, my remembrances of the Greek influence upon Charleston are vivid. It may have been difficult to walk three blocks without encountering a Greek-owned corner store. These were entrepreneurs who found a niche in providing the staples of everyday life to peninsular Charleston. They built other fledgling businesses, as well. In fact, my very first job was as the flower box custodian for a successful Greek florist on Calhoun Street. The refrigerated flower containers had to be kept clean, and I was always there on time to do the work for fifty cents each Saturday morning. I was only nine years of age. They surely overpaid me. The flower shop was barely a block from my childhood home.

My parents and grandparents often did business at a Greek-owned pharmacy on King Street. An upscale Greek shoe store was a fixture on King Street, as well. The finest heart surgeon in the region was Greek. Other Greek-lineage Charlestonians became architects, physicians, realtors, and restaurateurs. The generations of Greeks became part of the fabric that is Charleston. For sure, the free enterprise system was not taken for granted but celebrated by Charleston's Greek community. We slowly turned them into Geechee Greeks. Or did they convert us?

What I most remember as a youngster were those charismatic little corner stores. My brother Danny had a paper route up near Montague Street where a regular crowd gathered in the afternoon. They could have been Charleston Navy Yard workers or a shift from the State Ports Authority. It was as if that little corner store started a social club that met every workday afternoon. My brother would buy a Dr. Pepper for a nickel after we delivered his afternoon papers. That little hangout was where we met at the end of the route. I remember the owner dumping the Burger Beer bottle caps onto his side-yard driveway as a paving resource—much like one would use crushed oyster shells today. He had a thriving business. He was not unlike most of the Greek grocers of the 1950's and 1960's.

At one time there were nearly eighty of these charming grocers on the peninsula. And every one of them had a different personality. The one that was two blocks down at Vanderhorst and Rutledge also served as a butcher shop. The one on Beaufain Street was a candy store with the best comic book display in town. The one at Coming Street and Calhoun had a wide variety of pipe tobacco. And the one up at Queen Street even had a few small toys! There was also a wide array of fruits and vegetables from one block to the next. Fresh fruit was nature's candy.

Mr. Tony Creticos operated the closest Greek grocer to us, at the corner of Calhoun Street and Rutledge Avenue. It was the one I saw nearly every day. My mother was like other Charlestonians before refrigeration. They bought what was needed that day for the meals of the household. Waking up early, she would often send me to the Creticos store to pick up oatmeal or corn flakes. Mr. Creticos was a diminutive man, thin and quiet. He wore a fresh white full apron and kept a long stick with a grabbing mechanism that would reach the top shelves, usually ten feet above. He was continually restocking items on the shelves and rotating his inventory to the front. He was grandfatherly and spry. When I'd report the morning order, he would get the stick, grab the corn flakes and take a hand duster from his back pocket, delivering a spotless box to the brown paper bag. "And what else?" he'd always ask. It was as if he would lead you into filling the bag. "That'll be nineteen cents, son."

Mr. Creticos had a mechanical cash register. He'd punch a ten on one row and a nine on the other to show nineteen cents in the glass window. Then he'd toss the coins into the curved wooden slots. There were no receipts for a small order. He would utilize an order pad for larger purchases. A customer would simply come to the counter and rattle off what was needed. His small order pad was kept in his front apron pocket along with a pencil he kept sharp with his pocketknife. The pencil had a home behind his ear. The shavings fell upon the concrete floor, which was swept and mopped daily. Old whirring ceiling fans were utilized as needed in the Charleston heat.

Sometimes I would have a penny or two after school and go to the Creticos grocer to buy a Mary Jane or a Jawbreaker. Oddly, he would instruct those purchasing candy to drop the pennies into the candy and pick up what was purchased. He would collect all the pennies from the candy counter at day's end. His candy counter was a series of slanted rows—utilizing the boxes that the candy was bulk-packaged into to keep the display both neat and delectable to the neighborhood children. What he did not have were baseball cards. I bought those at the adjacent corner—at Oakman's Drugstore. Had the Creticos's grocery invested in baseball cards when I was about nine, Mr. Creticos might have retired much earlier!

The Greek influence is undeniable—they have thrived in the Holy City. They made Charleston better. And with their remarkable successes, many were able to do as I did— visit Greece in the thrill of travel to see where it all began.

Rear view of Old Exchange Building and Provost Dungeon.
Photo by author.

CHAPTER 39

Charleston from Years of Yonder

L OOKING BACK TO the two generations we are apt to have known as children gives us a perspective. It delineates what our grandparents and parents experienced to get us to the present. To build that foundation will require looking back a full century.

A century ago, Charleston was in a transitional stage. The repairs and reconstruction from the great hurricane of 1911 had mostly been completed. That 1911 hurricane killed seventeen people here—sadly—and was generally cited as the catalyst for the loss of rice plantations in the Lowcountry.[90] It was the tidal surge that purged the levees with saltwater. Though another hurricane also made a Charleston landfall in 1913, Charleston escaped the tragedy of further deaths. Hurricanes came on short notice back then. We now have amazing advancements that give us reasonable warning, but there is nothing to prevent them. They keep lining up each summer to march into the disaster lottery of the Gulf of Mexico or the eastern coast of the United States. We sometimes get in the way.

Besides the constancy of disaster repairs, other construction in Charleston we readily recognize today began in 1913. It seemed to be a year when there were plenty of cheap bricks on the market. Transitions will always need more bricks. St. Francis Xavier Infirmary began in 1913, later to become St. Francis Hospital—and now Roper-St. Francis Hospital. That old hospital at Ashley Avenue and Calhoun Street was run efficiently by the Sisters of Charity of Our Lady of Mercy. I knew them well. I was an altar boy at the daily Mass in their chapel. They also taught young ladies vying for certified nursing degrees until 1968. My older sister, Gail, was in their last graduating class.

In other hospital news of a century ago, the state took over the Medical College and its original building on Queen Street—by constructing a new building on Calhoun Street (completed in 1914).

The state appropriated $10,000 for that purpose or about the cost of today's anesthesia.

One hundred years ago identified a period of other resourcefulness. Did we manufacture uniforms in the old jail? Yes, we did. The city's spooky Old Jail was built in 1802,[91] but hit its stride after the atrocities of slavery and the Civil War prisoners incarcerated there. The jail was built initially to house arriving immigrants, but it seems that criminal activity in Charleston was on the rise. By the beginning of America's entry into World War I (1917), it was utilized as a military service uniform factory. Now it serves the Holy City's tour guides as a prominent place for disturbed spirits from the great beyond. I've never seen one, but then again, they are invisible.

The city's first skyscraper, the People's Building, had already been opened by 1911. It featured the nuance and curiosity of an indoor elevator, complete with an operator. When President William Howard Taft visited this monstrous yellow-brick skyscraper, he rode the state's first installed elevator to the roof and pronounced what he saw as 'the most magnificent view in all of America.' Charleston pundits agreed that it was surely a great view, but not likely the best in America. It was, however, the best view in Charleston because it was the only view without that ugly yellow-bricked People's Building skyscraper in it.

Charleston was still in the steep decline initiated by what those living Charlestonians in the early 1900's described as "that recent unpleasantness." Yet there was optimism for the future. The U.S. Navy placed a few jobs in the area by 1904 with the eventuality of funding a major shipyard to complement one of the East Coast's most vital naval bases. By 1910, housing starts in North Charleston (unincorporated) and surrounds were anticipating much more. But those sailors found out how to get downtown. Our era of night tourism had started. We had nightly incidents of broken bottles, broken jaws, and broken curfews. As a submarine base, the prospect of nuclear power and extensive weaponry stockpiled did not seem to excite locals as much as cruise ships and market area visitors without proper attire. Ironic, huh?

Ah, fashion! The zipper was invented in 1913. It's still better than Velcro. It's hard to believe it has only been around for a century. Our poor grandparents had to button up. Tiered dresses, bodices, and hats were in vogue. Guys had a pocket watch pocket. It's because there were no wristwatches. The millennial generation has no need of a watch. It's on their smartphone along with a few hundred other gadgets.

The world around Charleston was tumultuous by 1915. Albania had become a country. There were tensions in the Balkans (two wars), in Mexico, in China, and in the Philippines. Another war started between Bulgaria and Romania. The Turks and the Greeks had a sea battle near Troy. Yes, that same Troy from antiquity. They never learned. A year earlier, the Balkans produced another fire-starter in Sarajevo with the assassination of Arch Duke Ferdinand. The Great War (World War I) resulted.

Despite all the world tensions, the pace of life in Charleston barely changed in the 1910s. We managed ourselves as if quarantined from much of the progress afar. No subways were being built, no oil barons investing, and no new industry to hoist our spirits. There were just the aging veterans from the Civil War and the spunkier ones from that 1898 clash with Spain. Our old homes continued to be whitewashed and repaired as other forward-thinking cities demolished and rebuilt. America of the Industrial Age had pretty well passed us by. We languished. We had no idea that this was our most propitious era. What we could not afford to tear down and replace defined our future.

When the soldiers came back from the Great War in 1918, they were greeted with a worldwide pandemic. In fact, history tells us that more U.S. citizens died from the 1919 pandemic than from the battlefields of Europe. It had to be a sad development heaved upon a tragic city still trying to find its glorious past.

Charleston, it seems, was spinning in its solitude and looking for something on the order of an oil or gold discovery. The lament of the past still persisted, fifty years after the end of hostilities between the North and the South.

The lethargic pace of recovery did indeed stymie growth and prosperity. The decline was not only in the economy but also in an implicit attitude of the struggle.

The moon tides may wash upon our streets, and our traffic condenses upon roads built for horses—but the world has since found us. And a hundred years from now, our old stuff will be older yet.

Rooftop cocktails and dining at the Market Street Inn.
Photo by author.

CHAPTER 40

Culinary Customs and Hypes

THE CULTURE OF cooking has arrived. Charleston, especially, has an optimistic case of culinary one-upmanship. We're trying to seduce the connoisseurs. We Geechee-cook.

"Food fashion" is simmering across the globe—from Bali to Maui, from Vienna to Venice. What was for centuries a necessity of preparation and delivery is now an art. It's even called the culinary arts. It's like when the spaghetti sauce boils over and pops onto the kitchen wall. Don't clean it up; leave it. That's also a culinary art. Or it could be pop art, as well.

The food preparation transition may have been anticipated in the past decades just within the décor of kitchens. Double-ovens and stainless grill tops with range hoods are the rule. And men came in and made their mark. Women were getting home from the office late. Chefs with Pillsbury Doughboy hats appeared out of nowhere. They found new joy in cloves, braises, and sautés. Secret recipes were locked in the safe. Grilling contraptions that brought drunken chickens and Boston Butts to football tailgates sometimes exceeded the cost of the vehicle that hitched them hither.

The barbecue culinary culture is only a small part of the new cooking sciences. There are mustard-, vinegar-, and tomato-based varieties of barbecue. There is even the waft of Creole. Barbecue grills have taken over the world, from Australia to Alaska. I have two brothers who own barbecuing equipment that's worth more than my 401k-retirement plan.

Cuisine is on a heightened platform.

There are people that match wine with foods. The grand sommelier has arrived. These wine experts make wine suggestions. They will be around for a few centuries because they are planting vineyards in Croatia, New Zealand, and Morocco. Just a few short years ago the wine wars were between Napa Valley and the Burgundy region of

France. Great wines are coming out of China, Chile, Italy's Tuscany region, and Spain. Australia has begun their winery surge, as well. It's a growing industry in Germany and South Africa, as well.

Free-range meats are the rage. There are chickens and turkeys, bison and cattle. Evidently, somebody took the fencing down. There are menus all over the world bragging about the free-range entrées. However, you can bet somebody is paying taxes on that land. Don't be fooled. Nothing's free.

Reduction sauces are being advertised as the new rage. I've tried at least a dozen of them around Charleston and didn't lose one stinkin' pound.

Even salads are getting fancy. Some people make them with things that are not lettuce. How can that be? A waitress talked me into the newest fancy salad on a local bistro menu recently. After a bite or two, she stopped by to make sure I was brought into the world of new-age salads. I have a habit of being honest. It wasn't anything I expected to eat and was, to my rudimentary palate, repulsive.

"It tastes like a combination of beach sand, and a red ant pile wetted down by rancid vinegar," I replied.

She brought me a plate of fries. Check, please.

I guess I'm the meat and potatoes unsophisticated guy they should keep out of the finer establishments. Visa and Mastercard have already asked me to stay home. But the exciting world of cuisine I never knew as a child is upon us all. Charleston has restaurants that would compete favorably with the best in San Francisco, New Orleans, and New York. One could change eateries for a fortnight and never encounter a meal less than superb. We're in the right place.

To wit, we have freshwater fishing entrees and "off the hook" deep-sea delicacies, local farms, bakeries, and pastry shops. We have chocolatiers and confectionaries. We've attracted top chefs and stocked impressive wine cellars. We have cultural foods from every corner of the globe—French, Indian, Mexican, Chinese, African, Greek, and Italian. We even have excellent kosher choices. There is an amazing array.

Charleston has come a long way since we natives adjusted to a beneficial consequence. We just kinda figured that those coming here would eventually become hungry.

GEECHEE MEANDERINGS

Charleston Mayor Joseph P. Riley, Jr., met Charleston's
greatest modern challenges for forty years.
Photo by author.

CHAPTER 41

Meet Joe Riley

PERHAPS A HUNDRED years from when the last of these overstocked books are sold at a garage sale, visitors to Charleston will hear the name Joe Riley as if he were Louis XIV or Daniel Boone. He's bigger than that. Joseph Patrick Riley, Jr., served as the mayor of Charleston from 1975 to 2016. His forty years trumped the previous four hundred.

The slightly built visionary was educated at local schools before subscribing to higher education at The Citadel (Class of 1964). After earning his law degree at the University of South Carolina, he came back to fold into the multitude of seersucker suits on Broad Street where Charleston lawyers pass each other and say "howjado."

Riley was elected to the South Carolina Legislature before he turned thirty. But his S.C. House District had a more compelling and sudden need. Another long-serving mayor, Palmer Gaillard, accepted a position as undersecretary to the U.S. Navy. An interim mayor kept the office lights on until a special election could be arranged. Destiny won!

But what Riley had won was not what anyone would get too excited about in 1975. Charleston had boarded up vacancies throughout the city. The police department had just experienced its latest embarrassment, and the infrastructure was thought to be unfixable. The streets were not safe. Vibrant tourism was still a dream of someone else's tomorrow.

The man had a plan. He focused on bringing Charlestonians back to the peninsula for their shopping and entertainment. His multi-faceted vision would take time, patience, and funding the city did not have available.

He needed a new look at the police department. Check. He needed a better process for city planning. Check. He needed to build confidence in those that would come to see Charleston by making it the rose it once was—more than a hundred years prior. Check.

What he really needed was the confidence of the citizenry to be a part of the transition. His extraordinary podium presence attracted "buy in." He was magic in a bottle. And he would defer any compliment. The nexus of timing and luck conspired as well.

An event walked into city hall, and it spoke Italian.

An established international maestro, Gian Carlo Menotti, had been touring parts of the United States in search of a setting for an arts festival. Arts? *We do dat.* Menotti found the smaller venues like churches and community meeting halls to be most suitable for the enterprise. Spoleto USA was born. In time, people came from places unknown on many Old-World maps to a place of relative anonymity—Charleston. Arts drew an international following. It was just what Charleston and Joe Riley needed.

By 1986, Charleston's first full-service five-star hotel opened (then as the Charleston Omni; now the Belmond). That hotel had babies.

Other events upped their game like the Southeastern Wildlife Exposition, the Cooper River Bridge Run, Piccolo Spoleto, MOJA Arts Festival, Family Circle Cup, and the Lowcountry Oyster Festival. In time, there was rarely a weekend on the Charleston events calendar that was open. As an observer, it seemed that people came and saw the place, liked it, and returned. Some even stayed. The tourist industry boomed and zoomed.

Meanwhile, Joe Riley deferred the credit to everyone around him and smiled a knowing smile of an accomplished leader in a time when leadership mattered. He still lives downtown but never complains when the sanitation workers come late, or the college kids skateboard down his street. He loves this city more than anyone.

He is the consummate Geechee. That means cumyas cannot fully understand him—as they would not likely understand me. But we Geechees understand each other. Of all the treasures that Charleston espouses, Joe Riley is the one central to it all.

Shrimp boats align for the next morning's
adventure at old Shem Creek circa 1952.
Over the years, the restaurants replaced the shrimping fleet.
Watercolor by Charlotte Simmons McQueeney.

CHAPTER 42

Going, Going, Gone
with the Wind

G ONE WITH THE Wind (1939) has been accorded by many movie aficionados as the best movie ever screened. Accordingly, Geechees are often asked: "Is Charleston in Gone with the Wind?" Well, yes. No. Yes and no. Okay no is the best answer.

None of Gone with the Wind (GWTW) was filmed in Charleston unless the general opening scenes of the Old South are included. There, one would see Boone Hall Plantation in Mount Pleasant.

Blasphemy, you say!

The fictional character Rhett Butler (played by Clark Gable) was from Charleston, and at the end, he says he's "Going back to Charleston." Smart guy.

To say that Charleston is mentioned several times would be accurate. But that's a technicality. GWTW was filmed almost in its entirety in California. Even the scenes of Atlanta burning were done in Tinseltown. No matter where it burned, they rebuilt it. They had to have a home for the Braves and Falcons, right?

One of the eight main actors for GWTW was, in fact, a Charlestonian. And that lady's name? Rhett! Alicia Rhett. She was a tall stage actress at the Dock Street Theatre when she was discovered and asked to play the role of Melanie Wilkes. She had the perfect accent, unlike Vivien Leigh (who played Scarlett O'Hara). But when the young Alicia Rhett showed up in Hollywood, the producer, David O. Selznick, noted that she was too tall. She played the role of Melanie's sister, India Wilkes, instead. It was her first movie.

Alicia Rhett was an accomplished portrait artist and painting was her first love. She never acted again. But she produced an excellent portrait of my grandmother that hangs proudly in my home today. I knew Ms. Rhett and attended her funeral in 2014. She died a month short of turning ninety-nine.

For many years, it was rumored that the dashing Rhett Butler was modeled after the real Charleston entrepreneur James Adger. Adger was into shipping, high finance, and was just rich enough to coddle historic attention. The author of the novel, Margaret Mitchell, explained in interviews that she had no historical model for Rhett Butler. She made him up. Authors can do those kinds of things. The good ones can even be believable.

In summary, if some young coed tour guide with a Boston accent approaches you at the City Market and asks if you want to go on a GWTW tour, ask if it's a direct flight because there is no basis for a Gone with the Wind tour in Charleston. If the young lady steps forward and says, "Please. I need you to book this tour. I need the money to pay for my tuition in the fall." Repeat after me, "Frankly, my dear, I don't give a damn."

Church Street walk is the way to the market and
the famous Charleston establishments.
Photo by author.

CHAPTER 43

Pub Crawling Until Laid Flat

SOME FOLKS COME in for a weekend conference and throw caution to the wind. The winds near me have so much discarded caution that I have to duck often.

Charleston started as Charles Towne (and variously "Charles Town") and the ships coming here had bills of lading that were laden with spirits for a thirsty crowd. They brought wine, beer, and rum. In early Charleston, we mixed these three and called it a holy fiddler crab. Once you had four of these, you'd be likely to walk sideways.

We built homes, churches, meeting halls, and schools. Then we started to build pubs. The oldest of these is the Pink House on Chalmers Street. It dates to 1709.[92] It was a tavern, and it was busy. The Pink House Tavern has a Bermudian or Barbados-style of architecture. The swashbucklers drank there, and so did brass knucklers. There were brawls and donnybrooks. The donnybrooks were from the Irish sailors since the origin is their word for the town of Donnybrook. It means "free-for-all." It wasn't. The drunken sailors never worried about lodging because the jailer had a bed waiting.

By the time that the Quakers (Society of Friends) arrived in Charleston (1681),[93] more taverns were being built. Many of them left for Pennsylvania in 1685. The Quakers were on the puritanical side of morality and did not frequent the local pubs. When they left, Charleston had the ratio of a pub for every eleven citizens. Holy palmetto bugs!

The current ratio is a bit larger, but there are noteworthy places for pub crawls throughout the peninsula. Personally, I'd start at the top. Try the rooftop at the Vendue Inn. Once the harbor air enchants, view the surrounds to map the route toward the next specialty concoction. Tommy Condon's has live Irish music. Near there, try the O-Bar at the Charleston Oyster House. We're still walking straight. The Griffon brings in locals and visitors alike. You like elegance? Try Victor's Social

Club on the Alley next to Michael's on the Alley (fine steaks). Check out the artwork. If you would like a nightcap before you call Uber, try the rustic old bar at Husk. It's cozy, pricy, and might be near your hotel.

Some of the high-end restaurants have higher end bars. Hall's Chophouse has a fine bar, but as Yogi Berra used to say, "Nobody goes there anymore because it's too crowded." 39 Rue de Jean has a similar experience. The rooftop at the Market Street Pavilion is one of my personal favorites because of the view.

The Geechees know what bars used to be warehouses and abandoned buildings. Just ask. We can make up a celebrity-sighting story as eloquently embellished as any of the finest bartenders in Manhattan. Only ours are more likely to have a real moved-here (cumya) celebrity in it.

There are private places to have a drink or two, but the memberships encourage guests. It is part of the Geechee welcoming package. The most famous of these is the Hibernian Society Back Bar. You can't buy a drink there. But your member host can. That's a bonus for you. The South Carolina Yacht Club also has a welcoming membership and a famous atmosphere for a toddy. Never pass up these invitations.

The newer hotels are emplacing their own gorgeous establishments. It seems that another is opening each week.

As a truth-in-lending-type disclosure, I should mention that although I am not a teetotaler, I am a barely qualified social drinker who would be most unlikely to partake in a pub-crawl. I would more likely be your designated driver. But I have been to the places I recommend.

If you can't have a grand time in Charleston, up your medications. It's near the end for you.

Oakman's Drugstore 1954.
Watercolor by Charlotte Simmons McQueeney

CHAPTER 44

Excavations Made Easy

I T SEEMS THAT every other week, a new "dig" is taking place in Charleston. It may be a pipe repair, a utility upgrade, or even an archeological exploration. We have an overabundance of holes to fill in the peninsular city.

In digging, we find our past and maybe even a few gems along the way! I have a Civil War-era cannonball to prove it.

It is propitious that our abundances are abundant. The history of subterranean cultivation has long gone underground. Let's further explore this cavernous subject.

Somebody somewhere looked up, looked around, and then looked down. They then dug a hole. It may be that the world's earliest excavator found clay—and made cups and pots and wine jars and bricks. Surely clay would be used for shelter. It was only a few millennia before pup tents. Once early mankind was able to sit in a clay hut or pueblo and laugh at a passing rainstorm, other ideas were unearthed. We're not too sure about when who found what where.

Charlestonians seem to attach the idea of discovery to the notion of necessity.

Where does the phrase salt of the earth originate? Salt was available early. The Carthaginians, Visigoths, and Romans crossed the Mediterranean to Formentera[94] (in the Balearic Islands) to find a way to augment tasteless popcorn. Salt was used to preserve meat, as well. It was a precious commodity before there were words like precious and commodity. What could be better than salt?

While salt became essential, bronze and iron ore became as popular as heavy metal music. These early metals were made into hand tools and then farming implements. The Sumerians could really get into a hoedown. There are no Sumerians in Summerville. Sumerians grew more veggies than they needed, and their neighbors were not polite enough to ask for the seeds. They opted to use the same metals to make weapons. The rest is history—literally!

Glitzy stuff was cast aside momentarily. Gold and silver outshined slaggy iron and curiously malleable copper. The glitzy metals were used to trade as if they were money. And then they became money. Oh dear! The envy of country clubs and posh vacation homes started right then! Some of that gold made its way to King Street jewelry stores.

Diamonds came much later than glass. Cubic zirconia was good enough for a few centuries. The glass came from the beach sand and really helped guys like Galileo and Copernicus. Copernicus was not named after copper. Glass also made it easier to see what concoction the Venetians were drinking all the way from Florence. The Venetians found glassware to be easier to assess cleanliness in the dishwasher than clay cups. For centuries prior to blown glass, the stain in the clay cup could have been any number of despicable substances.

Rubies competed with diamonds for a while but lost. Now they compete with emeralds and sapphires. Don't even get me started on amethyst. All of these stones had a rocky beginning deep within the early mines. No mines were found with these precious stones in the entirety of Charleston County. Mining never caught on in the pluff mud.

Other resources caused a groundswell. There was coal. We didn't need coal until snowmen needed eyeballs. Coal provided heat and eventually energy. It also provided an economy for West Virginia and Eastern Kentucky. Energy being a buzz-word of the Industrial Revolution, other commodities ensued. There was oil, crude at first, but eventually pretty slick. Then there was natural gas. Eventually, there was shale so that we could invent a word like "fracking." It can be used in polite company these days.

Other larger stones were found that looked nice on a mantel. We found some marble, limestone, and granite. We kept chiseling away until we had the Venus de Milo, the Colossus at Rhodes, and several weatherworn pyramids. The ancients were never bored, though they were frequently boring. They were boring into extensive mining veins and found that digging holes could help them with other ideas—like burying kings, hiding treasures, and in the case of the Chinese, building an entire underground army— the terracotta warriors of Xian. The G.I. Joe Corporation saw that example as something promising.

Speaking about boring into the earth, the Boer Wars had nothing to do with mining. Yet, where they were fought in the southern part of Africa mattered. It's the world's largest repository of diamonds.

Does anyone wonder what other resource is taken from the earth in quantities more than all others combined? Give up? It's right there before your very eyes. Dirt. Dirt is the most excavated commodity. It's frequently moved and reintroduced for other uses. We use it to fill in lakes, to level land, and to bolster our suburban lawns. It covers our refuse and shapes our roads. You can buy dirt these days inexpensively. It's dirt cheap. Dirt is not mined like other resources. It is merely extracted in an unrestricted and ungoverned manner. So, if the Australians take out too much, the world might wobble. Dirt in Charleston made back lawns out of muddy high tide areas before there were environmental rules and aerial photography.

We take water from the earth, too—from underground systems called aquifers. We had aquifers before we had aqueducts.

Aqueducts were built to transport water over great distances. You could leave them out in the rain—no problem! There are no known underground aqueducts. They call those culverts.

We see the evidence of other problems under the topsoil. Our past is riddled with poorly engineered excavations. We have poked around a little too much in places we should not be poking. It's like we did these things in total darkness. There are swiss-cheese places underground in locales that have many Swiss people above ground. Don't worry, although Charleston has sinkholes—they are few, by comparison.

One would think that with all of these mines the earth above would sink. In fact, there are tremendous sinkholes across the globe. One in Egypt is fifty miles by seventy-five miles wide![95] That's a whole lot of "watch out!" Three of the world's top ten sinkholes are in Texas and Pennsylvania. Blame oil and coal.

Taking stuff out of the earth lets the air rush in. Air has very little structural support. Perhaps there could be appropriate places for public landfills, after all.

In summary, it really makes sense that we keep taking things out of the earth, and then we dig down to find past civilizations. I suppose they all fell into ancient sinkholes. Over time, we should put a few things back.

Charleston City Hall. Designed by architect Robert Mills.
Mills was the architect for the Washington Monument.
Photo by author.

CHAPTER 45

Geechee List of Instruction for Life

I T TOOK ME years and even decades to resolve the immortality issue. When I was thirteen, I thought the sun came up to make my day warm, and the moon came out so that I could look up. I had the only brain that had ever resided in my body. How could it fail me during all of those years? The civilization around me had to be about getting me through as the only immortal. Right?

Eventually, I found out with considerable disappointment that mortality had me marked in time. It must've flashed up at Times Square just before midnight. "Dummy, look up. Pay attention. Observe. You're on borrowed time."

It was a narcissism exorcism.

I began to look deeper, listen intuitively, and sense things more profoundly. My enjoyment of all things increased exponentially. I found truths and insights. I'm not talking about being born again or standing on a mountaintop—though that would have clearly explained my clouded vision.

I'm talking about discovering human nature in the kaleidoscope of humor, sensitivity, and reasoning. I did not descend upon a waiting crowd with chiseled tablets, but I did bring back the precepts of underlying joy to enrich anyone's life. All I did was follow the guidelines of the Geechee life. What made us a bit different while we were waiting for a century for someone to notice?

The observations have enhanced my drift toward senior citizen status. Perhaps I will grow the beard of Methuselah and someone will ask me to divulge these principles. Okay, twist my arm.

I did write things down and save them in a box. I still have that box. It sufficed before there was such a thing as a hard drive backup. One

Saturday when the rain prevented other priorities, I began cleaning my office to re-organize it. I came across that old box. I took the old notes, the ditties, and the profound sentencing from the scraps of paper and entered them by category into my computer. I realized that I had more than a dozen observations. I placed them in a readable order.

The Geechie List of Instructions for Life

1. Lend your most cherished asset to a stranger in need—your smile. It could disrupt the coldness of a life in need of warmth.
2. Unsolicited acts of anonymous and spontaneous charity will change the fortune of another and move your soul tenfold.
3. Engage in communication with someone you haven't spoken to in a year or more. It matters. Friends are your best collection in life.
4. Listen to your emotions. Tears come from both sadness and happiness. They are the mortar of mankind.
5. Open and clear views never include the spot where you're standing. Imagine another's perspective before making your opinion known.
6. Humble and sincere service to humanity is the only antidote to the tendency of arrogance. Arrogance has no standing in society.
7. Imagine how your triumphs could benefit others. Your good fortune could develop an opportunity to enhance another's happiness, as well.
8. Never find excuses to give up. The light behind the next door may be celestial.
9. Share a quiet sunset. That simple joy is greater than all the world's riches.
10. Make trauma internal to the degree it does not lessen the optimism of others. It is the most selfless gesture you can offer.
11. Always stoop to see into children's eyes at the equal height of the world in which they live. It prioritizes them and brings you back to an innocence of things you never imagined.

12. Dream a dream. All art, culture, and science grew from dreams that dreamers dreamt. Share it into reality.
13. Prayer works. The fact that there is a prayer offered always makes adversity tenable. Prayer is the strongest silence known.
14. Laugh. And then laugh again. Laughter makes your heart leap beyond the bounds of gravity. There is exuberance in laughter. We can only laugh with the conviction that joy is in our heart. Laughter is the best remedy for every malady known within our sphere.

The great iron skillet banged my noggin hard enough to knock my world askew. Being an unpretentious nobody is good. Understanding that we are mortals who can transfer hope to others gives us a speck of immortality.

We should always keep a trunk full of earned humility.

Benyas seem to know these things from our shared isolation. A cumya can become an Honorary Geechee Benya by following the Geechie List of Instructions.

East Battery home with carriage house in rear. These Charleston "double houses" are mansions.
Photo by author.

CHAPTER 46

Charleston, America, and the World

WHO ARE WE? We're the world together, the countries separated, and the cities within. There are some forests and farms and islands and deserts. Even Geechees realize Charleston is just a teeny tiny spot in the world we live. We have to get away from ourselves to see the big picture.

The two American continents have been both isolated and protected for five hundred years. Upstarts once, the United States of America is now the one civilization that the rest of the world touts as a barometer. We can foretell the coming times by our massive impact upon monetary markets, natural resources, and military mindset. There is ample and constant barometric pressure.

The objective look at world statistics places us where we really are! Based on a concept of measurement called an economist intelligence unit, the United States ranks seventeenth in the world for what we produce in our most important factory—our schools.[96] Our graduation rates, methods, and testing results are all a part of the measurement. Not surprisingly, the funding we push at education is but a minor factor. As they say, you can't just throw money at the problem. We need to study other countries that have succeeded like Finland, Switzerland, and South Korea.[97] It is education that advances society. Geechees know that!

Interconnected global concerns are going forward. For instance, we remain the juggernaut of the economic world. We are much larger than second-place China's gross domestic production total. But one only has to glance at the EU (European Union) to note the precariousness. The EU out-GDPs us. The EU landmass is nearly half of the U.S. All ten of the most generous countries in the world (per capita) are members of the EU. So, the EU as a conglomeration of nations has become a major economic player in the world. But eight of the top ten tax rates for countries are EU, most over 50 percent! Looking for a break? Try Singapore at a top rate of 20 percent.[98] Or you can pay 62 percent in Britain, old chap. Geechees can't pay that.

Russia has less than half of our population. India has tripled our population, and it is still less populous than China. What country is closest to our population measurement? That's right, Indonesia. They have a whopping 250 million people across those steamy Pacific islands. Been there. There are too many families on mopeds. Pakistan, the sixth largest population in the world with nearly two-hundred million people has been a receiver of billions of support from us.[99]

Throwing money at what has been historically dysfunctional is a precarious plan. We have given over $10 billion every year just to countries in the Middle East.[100]

Poverty? The top ten impoverished nations are all in Africa.[101] We send money, food, medicines, and technology—as do others from developed nations. We have our own poverty. But the definition differs. Our impoverished are rarely starving, diseased, and unsheltered. We have safe drinking water and so many government programs that it is nearly impossible to be considered impoverished in the same terms as may be used in Africa.

Where are the highest crime rates per 100,000 of population? Iceland, Sweden, and New Zealand—all developed countries—top that list. In the U.S., we'll approach twelve million crimes in a year,[102] And that does not include parking meter violations. By comparison, India will have less than two million crimes per year. Remember, they are three times our population! Charleston is an isolationist study. Crime in the Holy City has had a poor showing—and that's good!

There are many places to go to be murdered, but you should not have guessed the Land of the Free. The worst murder rate is in Honduras. You might not want to stop in El Salvador on the way. They're second. Others? Colombia, South Africa, and Venezuela. The United States didn't make the top 25.[103] Law and order are still in style.

The United States remains as our planet's most powerful nation and holds the world's biggest bag of switches.[104] Russia is next but has half our manpower and a tenth of our budget. We generally have two strong and reliable allies—the UK (no. 6) and Canada (no. 22).[105] The world's third strongest military power, you ask? China. They have plenty of personnel who have no first cousins. After India (no. 4) is France (no. 5). France—the place with all the table manners—has been on the rise. Germany is eighth.[106]

In measuring the quality of life, the U.S. only ranks seventeenth.[107] Canada, Denmark, and Sweden rate as the top three. Does crime pay? New Zealand—with its high petty crime—is the sixth highest quality of life place to live.[108] There are twenty times as many sheep in New Zealand as there are people. Whoever counted them slept that night.

Our national debt has made headlines in the last few years. We're in first place there. But the UK is not far behind at about two-thirds our debt. France and Germany are no. 3 and no. 4. Our debt reduction plan is simple—the US needs to win the lottery.

Are you hungry? We feed the world. Only France can boast with us of significant food exports. Our farmers are the best. Some of them live over John's Island way. John's Island tomatoes are scrumptious. Every Geechee knows about mader sam wishes.

Are there places where being number one can cast the largest shadow? Why yes! The U.S. is the most obese country on the globe. There are beefy Geechees, too. We need to export even more food and not keep as much available. Yet the U.S. is the leading world manufacturer of exercise equipment.

The illegal drug cultures that we know are scattered across the planet. Afghanistan grows 93 percent of the world's opium poppies. Colombia is the world's top cocaine supplier. Go figure. Alcoholism? We're back to Iceland, the world's number one. Russia's a drinking man's paradise. Beer? Germany and the Netherlands. Try the U.S. as well. Geechees? We like our liquor on the rocks and our beer from brewpubs. Wine goes with everything.

The world community raises a few eyebrows when it comes to statistics. But they rarely tell the whole story. There is very little crime in Singapore because there is no tolerance—even for minor disruptions. Public canings are real deterrents.

So, check the numbers. Pay your taxes (if you can). Keep your nose clean, and enjoy liberty.

I am not aware that there has ever been a jaywalking ticket given in Charleston, a city where it's rare to hear a car horn.

Charleston from Fort Johnson 1959.
Watercolor by Charlotte Simmons McQueeney.

CHAPTER 47

Solutions to Unforeseen Problems

IT MAY BE difficult to imagine, but Charleston had a negligible tourist industry in the 1950s and 1960s. They stayed away like bats from sunlight. After all, the city suffered from scant hotel rooms, eateries, and activities. There wasn't much one could find to entertain downtown, but there was always the excitement of a visit to the formal gardens. Magnolia Gardens, Drayton Hall, and Middleton Place have stood the test of time, but even they suffered from a lack of national recognition.

Charleston had plenty of old turn-of-the-century hotels. We weren't quite sure which century turned. Humidity became our companion. Air-conditioned hotels became increasingly important because one would not anticipate the sweltering heat in Charleston from June through September. It's stifling. With few air-conditioned rooms, a visitor was apt to stay for the day and then move on to a Howard Johnsons chain hotel along the highway with the ABC rule. ABC meant "anywhere but Charleston." We gave tourists very little reason to stay in the Holy City.

The lack of tourism didn't seem to bother the old Charlestonians. They had grown tired of folks from beyond telling folks from within how to do something their way. Instead, they liked when they hit the highway. America's Friendliest City was not always that friendly. I suppose the summer heat had something to do with it.

Before there were bed-and-breakfasts, there were rooms for rent. These were utilized by enterprising families to thwart even more depression during the Great Depression years. My parents would never have met had there not been rooms for rent. The first tourist-attracting full-scale proper hotel with air-conditioning in Charleston was not built until 1970. I know this hotel well. I spent the summer of 1970 as part of the vast labor force of Ruscon Construction Company at the Mills House Hotel. They overpaid me at $1.40 per hour. It was good money, and I needed it to pay what I could toward my tuition at The Citadel.

I had no idea that the Mills House would make such a lasting impact on my sleepy old city. It attracted the history tourist. Ironically, the hotel that was torn down to make way for the Mills House was the Mills House of the 1800s. A few elements including a staircase and the wrought iron railings were preserved for use in the new Mills House.

In time, with the completion of other modern and exquisite hotels on the peninsula, Charleston became an amazing tourist destination. It rivaled others—not only in the United States—but also across the world.

Charleston became so popular in the past dozen years that the cruise lines began to call. This became a quite controversial issue since the city did not have a proper cruise terminal. The peninsula had limited space, so the cruise traffic could bottle up other commuters. Furthermore, the old-time residents preferred not to have a cruise ship blocking the morning sun. You see—there is not much in Charleston as tall as a cruise ship.

The debates about hosting cruise ships became spirited. Eventually, a new terminal was commissioned for that purpose. But the adversarial sentiments continued. The merchants felt that cruise travelers brought little new revenue. Furthermore, the dress code for the downtown area would be considered much more elegant than most world cities. Cruise passengers wore T-shirts and shorts. Our South-of-Broad-Street sensibilities would not stomach too much of that!

There had to be a way to balance the cruise ship / harbor debates in my Charleston. And, by Jove, I think I developed a solution.

First, let's move the Yorktown aircraft carrier over to the windward side of the Morris Island Lighthouse. We should hoist the stately ship out of the water atop the rocky groin thusly stopping the erosion of Folly Beach. An aircraft carrier can erode the idea of erosion. With proper planning, we can build a footpath from the Yorktown to the Morris Island Lighthouse at low tide. The Yorktown, known as "The Fighting Lady" can become the iconic emblem of Charleston much like the Statue of Liberty and the Sydney Opera House. The groin area could be filled in with the silt and old boat anchors from our overdue harbor dredging and become the New Folly Beach extension, full of expatriated residents from the town of James Island. Folly Beach could grow to be as big as Manhattan.

Secondly, let's park the cruise ships across the harbor to the vacated Yorktown berth. We could bring in a half dozen at a time. With the new dredging, the big super-cruisers could come with travelers from all over the world. Would anyone still complain if those monstrous cities on the water were "over there?" Mount Pleasant would benefit, and the Patriot's Point complex would have a constant source of people who think they landed in Charleston.

Thirdly, let's move the Columbus Street Terminal that's full of those colorful shipping containers to the old naval base site at North Charleston. They'd love to have the state ports industry there, complete with all of the rail lines and container trucks— closer to the Interstate. That leaves both the downtown Charleston cruise terminal and tremendous open shoreline for other development. This creates a potential for a trillion dollars' worth of expensive waterfront condominiums and retail shops that require the occupants to either walk or use golf carts within. Splendid!

Everybody's happy!

As a safety valve, let's leave that high chain-link fence up at the downtown Columbus container yard. We can ferry over the passengers from Patriot's Point to that Charleston-side property to get a feel of Charleston while we look them over on a secret video monitor. We could replicate important Charleston establishments inside the enclosure— like Big John's Tavern, the Timrod Hotel, a diapered horse and carriage, a seersucker-suited Broad Street lawyer, and the Old Jail. We could build a Kiawah casino for extra tax revenue. We should also hire the border patrol training school to limit actual entrance into the Holy Land—I mean the Holy City. Owing to our reputation for hospitality, we'd allow those with collared shirts to visit the South Carolina Aquarium first. Once they proved to be receptive to us as opposed to dismissive, we'd allow them into our cultural mecca!

When all of this does happen, somebody pause for a moment by my old gnarly grave and say, "Hey, you were right! The whole area is better—Folly Beach is bigger, Mt. Pleasant has a bustling cruise ship revenue, North Charleston received the port income, and Charleston got the brunt of the tourist dollars without the brunt of the traffic." I'll rest in peace.

For now, Geechee thinking is still alive.

New Year's Day Polar Bear Swim event at Sullivans
Island attracts 20,000 "crazies."

CHAPTER 48

The Scintillation

IMAGINE. LET'S EXPLORE the idea that you are visiting Charleston for the first time. She is a princess from antiquity. You had no idea that she would be stately, spirited, and bright. She is demure, yet spontaneous. You are her prince. You want to spend that very first day from dawn to dusk discovering what she is really like. A romance is surely possible.

It is within the great cities that magnificence abides. It is where the profound revelations arise. Dreams become imaginings that become ideas. Our Charleston is the muse of the many, the stage of the astonished, and the haven of the heartened.

Creativity glows. They are the back alleys that enlighten the casual stroller into boulevards of inherent beauty. The ambulatory luster is best in the pre-breakfast hour. Those that saunter and jog with those that stroll and walk the family pet—they all are up to view the soft light of the sun on the horizon and hear the yawn of an ageless city as it awakes.

There is chivalry within the pursuit of a city's charm and ambiance. The fantasies, the wishes, the delights, and the ideals associate within the seeming triviality of unplanned conversations, unprompted expressions, and unbridled inspirations. Fine cities lift people to the simultaneous pursuit of self-emergence and the heightened quest for a happier fate. The next dark corner or the single house with the porch light draws one's attention. The college kids and young mothers are seen in the fitness centers, coffee shops, and the bookstores. Some converge in the defiance of the routine. They seek the unknown turns of a life unchartered and uninhibited. Youth exhilarates.

Businesses bustle forth. Generations gather and cultures cluster to emerge and entwine like the thrush of yellow jasmine upon the lattice. The set dominance of myriad professions dart for their allotted time upon the cityscape. A car is parked in a space reserved. A seersucker suit appears. Perhaps they extoll their Geechee-ness for the fullness of the day, and then they go home. One wonders what providence lurks?

Urbanity breathes. The soft wind carries the moments of reflective and insightful visualizations upon park benches, bus stops, and garden views. The murmur of significance graphs a bearing from any seemingly inane moment of serendipity. Ambitions breed at the crossroads of the happy and the coincidental, at the nadir of a deep laugh, and at the tintinnabulation of church bells.

A good city will sweat. Inventiveness, resourcefulness, and originality may spring from the fortuitous fountain of a mannerly greeting or a mysterious encounter. Quiet impressions spray like a summer shower aimlessly. They drift across like the unknowing glance, the vis-à-vis, the head nod, and the shrug that hints, "Why me?" Cities are the greenhouses of the mystic and the exquisite. The simplicity of a minor satirical remark from a passerby may spur a design, a destiny, or a fortune. Perceptions spring forth to the porches and piazzas edified in the second glass of pinot noir. Relaxation was invented here. It arrived upon a warm ocean breeze from the southeast.

Colossal moments invariably ascend. Gentle words catapult a meaningful notion through unintended and unsolicited reaction. It has happened indubitably, at times innumerably. Pensively poignant personalities collide randomly. The arbitrary is preened from the unstructured and the unrehearsed. The Holy City is a mixture of the anonymous and the extemporaneous. They will marry the spontaneous and the impulsive. The casual occurrence intensifies from the inadvertent and unforeseen interaction of a voice, a face, and a smile. They become puzzled by enthralled with our Geechee-ness. It is like a secret that everyone knows but is still whispered.

The courteous greetings may seem pretended, but they are not. It is ingrained. The generosity is expected. The manners are the traditions unbroken. These are not the standards of every place but are the basics of this Old World community of etiquette purveyors—for they are the preservers of the cobblestone quadrants. The institutions welcome with receptive doormen, gregarious waitresses, and grin-toothed hostesses. They are rewarded for their attitudes.

But there are others. They may be Broad Street lawyers, ministers, the mayor, or charitable volunteers. Or they could be every man and every woman from the market to the Battery. With humility, they arise.

They want to show you their favorite part of their favorite port. They will likely show you their small courtyard garden and their old family joggling board. And they will explain us within our family lore. No one pays them. They do it because it is who they are.

Charleston is more than its history. Its stunning architecture is compressed within a lowland peninsula less than two miles square. It is the renewal of a state of mind, the expression of a pleasantly astounded newcomer, the ambiance of expected casual enjoyment—all welcomed with sincerity. It is melancholy mixed with nostalgia—those stonewashed memories lightened enough to lift the heart for a moment. The striations of refection last beyond the experience. The aftermath entails the longing lure for another day in its magnetic grasp. Charleston draws one in. Listen to the Geechee!

The evening breeds excitement cloaked in uncertainty.

The darkness becomes exciting and authentic. There are countless diversions—all ordained in the sense of the last discovery of the last moment of each day. It is the kiss goodnight by the princess.

All the high pursuits of life can be the tapestry inherent to a great city. Therein lies enchanted magic. Though our native population may sprawl to connected arteries, they will always drift back to the wrought iron, the tabby, and the slated sidewalks. We saunter forward to a new destiny by the dominance of azaleas and oleanders, palmettos and live oaks. The city lives heartily because it nearly died on too many occasions.

The full day's enchantment is poetic. Yet the next day promises another mystery and a new scintillation. Great cities are omnipotent and powerful potions. Our Geechee world is Charleston, and it is unlike any other.

Olde Charleston Brick

Masonry that meanders beyond the oleanders and cobblestone alleys
The church revivals, street-wise vendors, and political rallies
Sun drenched piazzas, ivy-walled courtyards and market arches
Bricks that breathe and cry and pulse and bow as eternity marches
Solid steps to the past, rekindle hope and plan tomorrow's residue
What they believed, they defended and would defend anew
Giving small credence to progress, denying it the respect of the ages
the rage of the wind, the roar of tides, the wrath that war wages
Buildings that trembled, then fell into repose beneath tin and slate
Bounded hard by the blackest of iron wrought into fence and gate
Shaded by palmetto and oak, time, temperance and pride
Warming resilient hearts that resisted then endured inside
Saltwater soaked mortar moors the assault of water and fire
A silhouette prominent with nature's reach and freedom's spire
Dominant upon the sun's retreat, casting its repressed light, stems
Upon its countenance, counting upon and depending on its sustenance
of masonry, of history, of life that meanders beyond the oleanders

This brick wall of prose was co-produced by the author
and his mother, Charlotte Simmons McQueeney.
Note that all lines end in a compass point.

Shem Creek 2012. Acrylic on canvas by the author.
Much has changed in the process of a burgeoning
tourism trade. It changed the creek.

EPILOGUE

IN THIS DAY of the conveniences—a desktop computer, a search engine, an email correspondence, and other digital enhancements—it makes no sense to not write it down. There are generations before me that I wish would have written it down. We would certainly be more informed—if not quite worldly. Our generation is particularly inspired to leave a legacy of information. Writing it down a generation ago meant whatever chiseled script one could afford to render upon a gravestone.

The predisposition of writing it down has emerged from an insight that Charleston had risen again. That was a prediction from my grandmother (Agatha Aimar Simmons, 1900-1982). It seems trite, but she never relinquished that noble belief.

I wrote other books. You could say that I wrote it down.

I was inspired because so many personalities made Charleston's resurgence possible. I sought the sources and scribbled their well-qualified perspectives. My first effort, The Rise of Charleston, was published in October of 2011. It was updated and re-published in 2017 at the request of the publisher, The History Press. Thirty-seven interviews examined the past for its effect upon our current status. We had arrived! I met Mayor Joe Riley for lunch, former Governor Jim Edwards for a morning chat, Judge Sol Blatt in his chambers on a quiet afternoon, and Congressman Arthur Ravenel, Jr., at his home on another morning. Actress-Artist Alicia Rhett smiled when I arrived at her retirement quarters. The effervescent Tim Scott met me at yet another lunch. I laughed with auto dealer Tommy Baker at his posh office and met Tommy Condon at the Hibernian Hall. Where else? School Board Chairman Hillery Douglas and his wife Yvette sipped lattés at a Starbucks. Former U.S. Senator Fritz Hollings talked about his childhood from the wingback chair at his office sitting area on Calhoun Street. The experience was unforgettable. Many of these personalities spoke in varying resonances with their Geechee-ness front and center.

Another book was in order. Sunsets over Charleston (2012) brought more interview-able personalities into the project. Another volume of stories to tell! There were more cumyas added—author Pat Conroy, actor Bill Murray, General John Rosa, and buoyant political personality Mark Sanford. But there were other benyas of profound local interest like project director Elizabeth Colbert Busch, singer Darius Rucker, golfer Beth Daniel, and Admiral Bill Schachte. To be sure, there are many more I did not interview that deserve mention, but my keyboard had encountered irregular palpitations! I had to stop somewhere.

All in all, the two books became a compendium of Charleston's recent history through the eyes of those who were largely responsible for the amazing upsurge. The books may have proved that we Charlestonians proudly persevered, that civility endured and that the visions of many grandmothers became reality.

A short book about a portion of Charleston's religious history was published in 2015, Holy Waters of Charleston. The book stretched my research abilities. The rest of my life will show the prominence of those stretch marks. Research is tedious and time-consuming. I'll leave it to the PhDs.

I slipped into formal literature. The year 2016 brought At First Averse and Then Another. It was a lifelong ambition completed. It featured my mother's artwork and mostly humorous scribbling from my view of the world as an observer. The verses were written not to be admired, but to be enjoyed. They represented a compendium of my life's jottings since I was thirteen. The companion book was published in the first quarter of 2017. Averse Again Now and Then added 231 other poems, all in the light-verse genre. The interior artwork interspersed is that of my own.

Recently, I had a novel idea. A novel! I had begun the process in early 2015 and completed Disaffections of Time (Xlibris Publishing) in April 2018. My gamble was that it would either grace the New York Times Bestseller List or flood the local garage sales market. Keep thou fingers entangled. I used many Charleston characters I had admired over a lifetime. My ageless fictional character (well, he's fictionally seventy-six) solves problems by piecing together trivialities to a constant clientele who visit him at a local coffee shop. There is intrigue, a few dastardly characters, and some uplifting portrayals of kindness. But the over-riding emotion is carried by a young romance of an unwed mother of twins and an amnesiac. Early review feedback online has been positive! The ending sets the book forward for a sequel.

The first book I started became the seventh book I completed. (That is, assuming that this volume is the eighth!) Around in Circles was begun in 2009 and completed for publication by late 2018, though the extensive edits (more research!) would take much patience. The book chronicles the incredible Forrest Gump-like life of a good friend, NCAA basketball coach Les Robinson. Robinson, a throwback rocking chair storyteller from the age before heightened media, was patient enough for me to get it all right. The book is punctuated with humor because that is his natural inclination.

What you may be holding by the weight of paper or a Kindle-like electronic device is also a completion, of sorts. In retrospect, it is the primer for everything else. In a small way, it surmises the wooded streams that became a river. In context, it is meant to capture the Charleston I have experienced for a lifetime and interpret it to the here and now. The production brought back warm remembrances and the perspective of being a witness to the miracle that is my city.

Even Geechee Gonna Gitcha has a sister book. It's the personal stories of my large family (I'm one of nine children) crammed into a four-room rental home in 1950s Charleston. Growing Up Geechee is meant to capture the insight of those times with humor and even a bit of inspiration. Growing Up Geechee wild follow closely behind Geechee Gonna Gitcha—distributed by the same publisher, Xlibris.

Every Geechee that ever was has made Charleston an amazing place. I salute the entire lot whether you understand them or not.

Here in the Holy City, there is an inevitable within an eventuality that is inescapable. A Geechee's gonna gitcha!

Author Tommy McQueeney rides off into the
next county on a procured equine.
Photo by Amanda McQueeney, wife of the author.

W. Thomas McQueeney

S INCE THE PUBLISHER asked me to write this myself, I had to tell the whole truth.

With some focused effort, I could have reached a level of under-achievement that may have redefined my uneventful life. I have enjoyed a lapse of non-responsive mediocrity that has obscured my ambivalence.

Upon high school graduation, I set out to change the world but found that I could not even change a bed sheet. I entered The Citadel so that my parents knew where I was at night. Shortly after graduation, I married too soon, had children in short order, and put everything on autopilot until I could get to the point of mindless nonchalance tempered by quiet boredom. My suspicions exceeded my uncertain skepticism.

A wind of change blew in a few years back. I bought a computer and learned MS-DOS by inserting floppy discs into a slot and then listened to what sounded like roaches moving in a frenzied scurry. I had made up my mind to learn something. I accepted the digital world. That new concept convinced me that there was life on the other side. I was afraid to open my computer, but I did spray a full can of Raid into the disc slot.

My life had nudged up to the idea of pending and foreboding ruin and public humiliation. I had to do something. I contemplated what would happen if I did nothing. Contemplation turned into slumber. The rest of my life has been an awakening without purpose. The doldrums happened within the confines of the interim times. There's a possibility that when I see old friends again, I could begin drooling, become incoherent, repeat myself, and repeat myself.

There has been no hobby, fascination, or passion that can possibly exceed my deep dedication to the spontaneous withdrawal from everything meaningful. I'm proud of my adequately timed power naps.

They don't bother anybody of significance unless one considers the driver behind me at the light.

One day some somber stone-faced person in a suit will be paid to direct a funeral to celebrate my life. If you have nothing else to do, stop by. I've left instructions that I should be set adrift in a hot air balloon. Anytime you see one, you can think about whether there are roaches in my computer.

I have but one slight change I've made that is significant since my birth. The very first gift I received when I came into this world that I could keep was a *W*. It began my name. I didn't think much of it at first, but by the time I reached college, having that W sounded important.

Prominent amongst the W's is W. Somerset Maugham, who wrote *Of Human Bondage*. That book sounds kinky, but it sold well enough to entice him to grow a mustache. Besides, what kind of idiot parent would name a male child Somerset? That kid probably got whupped by bullies every day on the way home from school. W. Somerset Maugham was not the first popular W in world history. That person might have been W. the Conqueror.

Dubya is such an excellent introduction to a name. Like Mr. Maugham, my *W* is for William. But leaving out the *illiam* is nearly poetic.

There are so many dubyas out there you probably already knew and liked. W. Disney. W. Chamberlain. W. Whitman. W. Jennings Bryan. W. Nelson. And, of course, W. Earp. How about W. Churchill and W. Shakespeare? They even made a movie about another Dubya. I think the name of the film was *W*.

I was fully named early in life. I had three of them with a suffix to boot. I had to use the first name for years instead of the name my parents called me. It was because the nuns that taught me had unchangeable habits. They didn't allow exceptions to the rule that your first name was your first name. Period. Actually, when the sisters finished me off, I adopted the period, too. My W comes with an automatic period behind it.

Not wanting to be confused with my father, who was able to use his formal William without concerns, I even dropped the suffix *Jr.* that was behind my name. Proud of my dad, I certainly did not want him to suffer from the high potential of my shortcomings. Besides, without the full first name and suffix, my name became easier to write on checks, mortgages, and parlay cards.

But now I'm older and have real responsibilities and an adult-like personality. Few people can discern the difference anymore. Since I'm closer to the other end of that "ashes to ashes" prophecy, I've decided I'd like to place a suffix back behind my name. I can't go back to "Junior." I never quite earned a PhD or an MD. I could be an esquire, I suppose. But lawyers use that one to let one another know that they are lawyers. That's a shame because I like the term *esquire*. It has a certain panache. Too bad I can't just put the word *panache* behind my last name.

It was during a sleepless night one day that I tossed and turned pondering the need of a suitable suffix. I just couldn't dream up the right one. Then—out of nowhere—a perfect suffix naturally came to mind. It would have awakened me in the excitement, but I was already up. The suffix came as suddenly as a belch after carbonated soda. Oops, I didn't mean to be so graphic. Voila! I have a new suffix that I will apply in the future so that everyone will know my name—even the guy next door that keeps calling me Tim.

I found a suffix with flavor, color, and the desire of all mankind. From henceforward, or just after the time of now, I will hereafter sign my name as "W. Thomas McQueeney, *au jus*." I think I first saw it on a menu. *Au jus*—it's just the extra succulence I needed for the rest of my life. The cannibal culture will love it. I think I'll be the first citizen allowed to leave the country to ever have it on a passport.

Thanks for finding out about me as an author. Author is a loose term that leads one to loose change, if things go very well.

I'm using the remaining pre-arthritic and pre-carpal tunnel time I have to write my memoirs. It's going to be titled Sporadic and Inconsequential Thoughts, the Large Print Edition. I'll know where I'm going with it when I get there. Meanwhile, the incredibly expeditious years of my demise await. Those days will define my grandchildrens' impressions of me forever.

Goodbye.

W. Thomas McQueeney, au jus

The Angel Oak. Johns Island is just south of the city.
Photo by author.

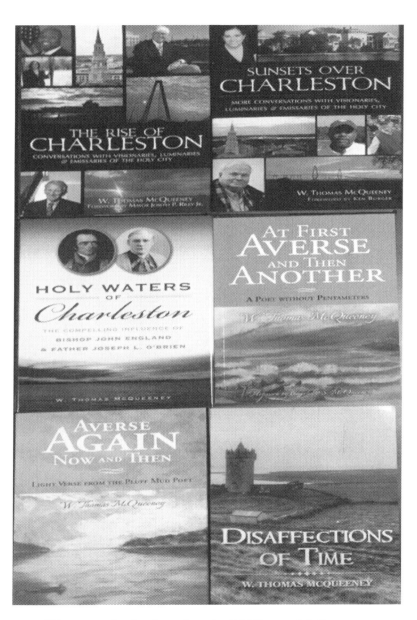

These are other books written by W. Thomas McQueeney. Available on Amazon and by title at most bookstores. **Coming Soon!** *Growing Up Geechee* (October, 2018) *Around in Circles: Les Robinson—Life, Basketball, and the NCAA* (November, 2018)

ENDNOTES

1   Charles I of England. https://www.royal.uk/charles-i-r-1625-1649

2   John Locke. https://www.britannica.com/biography/John-Locke

3   French Huguenot Church. https://www.huguenot-church.org/history.html

4   Siege of Charleston. https://lowcountrywalkingtours.com/2014/01/28/bombardment-of-charleston-1863-65/

5   Philomathean Society. http://www.charlestonfootprints.com/charleston-blog/charleston-social-traditions/2011/12/12/

6   Charleston Ugly Club. http://www.charlestonfootprints.com/charleston-blog/charleston-social-traditions/2011/12/12/

7   Charleston Ugly Club. http://www.charlestonfootprints.com/charleston-blog/charleston-social-traditions/2011/12/12/

8   St. Cecelia Society. https://www.questia.com/library/journal/1G1-3097 28112/secret-sharing-debutantes-coming-out-in-the-american

9   Oldest Societies. http://www.charlestonfootprints.com/charleston-blog/charleston-social-traditions/2011/12/12/

10   Frank Gilbreth, Jr. From the Column "Doing the Charleston."

11   Hurricane of 1786. https://charlestonlivingmag.com/storms-of-many-centuries

12   1790 and 1860 census data. https://www.censusrecords.com/content/1790_census

13   Metro area growth. http://www.crda.org/news/exactly-how-many-people-move-into-the-charleston-region-each-day/

14   Charleston Growth. http://www.crda.org/news/exactly-how-many-people-move-into-the-charleston-region-each-day/

15   Charleston Growth. Ibid.

16   Ordinance of Nullification. https://www.britannica.com/topic/nullification-crisis

17   James Pettigru. https://www.charlestoncitypaper.com/charleston/james-petigru-dared-to-challenge-confederacy/Content?oid=3245766

18   Earthquake of 1886. https://www.history.com/this-day-in-history/earthquake-shakes-charleston-south-carolina

19   Great Charleston Quake. Ibid.

20   Hurricane frequency. http://www.hurricanecity.com/city/charleston.htm

21   Hurricanes of Charleston. The entire group is taken from the following website: http://www.hurricanecity.com/city/charleston.htm

22 Chamber of Commerce. https://www.google.com/search?ei=_u7dWvq
    LDqa-jwSa1IHoAQ&q=Charleston+Trident+Chamber+of+Commerc
    e+history&oq=Charleston+Trident+Chamber+of+Commerce+history
    &gs_l=psy-ab.12...4162.5722.0.8623.8.8.0.0.0.0.118.795.4j4.8.0....0...1c.1.64.
    psy-ab..0.0.0....0.5wfATzs8qFQ

23 Quote from Mr. Michael Robinson, owner of Charleston Appraisal Service.

24 Post and Courier. http://charlestoncurrents.com/2016/09/history-the-post-
    and-courier/

25 Artesian Wells. http://www.charlestonfootprints.com/charleston-blog/well-
    wells/2012/02/01/

26 Artesian Wells. http://www.charlestonfootprints.com/charleston-blog/
    well-wells/2012/02/01/

27 Denmark Vesey revolt. http://www.blackpast.org/aah/denmark-vesey-conspiracy-1822

28 Chevaux de Frise. http://www.charlestonfootprints.com/charleston-blog/
    chevaux-de-frise/2011/02/24/

29 WCSC Television. https://en.wikipedia.org/wiki/WCSC-TV

30 Leslie Nielsen. https://en.wikipedia.org/wiki/Francis_Marion

31 Francis Marion. Ibid.

32 Francis Marion Hotel. http://francismarionhotel.com/press-releases/

33 Beauregard. https://www.civilwar.org/learn/biographies/p-g-t-beauregard

34 IBID.

35 PGT Beauregard. https://www.civilwar.org/learn/biographies/p-g-t-beauregard

36 Beauregard quote. http://www.nola.com/politics/index.ssf/2017/05/beauregard
    _confederate_monumen.html

37 Ghost of Room 10. https://www.hauntedrooms.com/10-haunted-places-
    charleston-sc

38 Ghost Soldier. Ibid

39 Lavinna Fisher. Ibid

40 Stede Bonnet. https://www.smithsonianmag.com/history/the-gentleman-
    pirate-159418520/

41 St. Philips Apparition. http://www.onlyinyourstate.com/south-carolina/
    ghost-stories-sc/

42 Edgar Allen Poe. https://www.gothichorrorstories.com/gothic-travel/historic
    -haunted-travel-destinations/in-old-charleston-the-historic-and-haunted-are-
    around-every-corner/

43 Abner Doubleday. https://www.biography.com/people/abner-doubleday-9277900

44 Abner Doubleday. https://en.wikipedia.org/wiki/Abner_Doubleday

45 Abner Doubleday. https://www.biography.com/people/abner-doubleday-9277900

46   Tuscarora Jack Barnwell. http://www.beaufortonline.com/tuscarora-jack-barnwell-founder-of-beaufort-sc/

47   Thomas Elfe. http://www.scencyclopedia.org/sce/entries/elfe-thomas/

48   Charleston Furniture 1680-1820. http://www.antiquesandfineart.com/articles/article.cfm?request=371

49   Heyward Washington House. https://www.ccpl.org/news/george-washington-charleston-1791

50   Eliza Lucas. http://www.elizalucaspinckneydar.org/?page_id=24

51   Eliza Lucas. http://www.elizalucaspinckneydar.org/?page_id=24

52   Eliza Lucas. Ibid

53   Eliza Lucas. Ibid.

54   Philip Simmons. http://www.craftinamerica.org/artists/philip-simmons/

55   Philip Simmons Quote. http://www.philipsimmons.us/aboutsimmons.html

56   Philip Simmons. Ibid.

57   Osceola. https://www.smithsonianmag.com/history/a-seminole-warrior-cloaked-in-defiance-60004300/

58   Osceola. Ibid.

59   General Jesup. https://georgia.gov/cities-counties/wayne-county

60   Osceola. https://www.smithsonianmag.com/history/a-seminole-warrior-cloaked-in-defiance-60004300/

61   William Gilmore Simms. http://www.theimaginativeconservative.org/2014/06/william-gilmore-simms-reading-list.html

62   Henry Timrod. https://www.poetryfoundation.org/articles/68697/bob-dylan-henry-timrod-revisited

63   St. Michael's Church. https://bulldogtours.com/bulldogbuzz/5-amazing-churches-in-charleston/

64   Unitarian Church. https://bulldogtours.com/bulldogbuzz/5-amazing-churches-in-charleston/

65   Beth Elohim Synagogue. https://www.10best.com/interests/heritage/fascinating-stories-behind-10-must-see-buildings-in-charleston-s-c/

66   St. Matthew's Church. https://en.wikipedia.org/wiki/St._Matthew%27s_German_Evangelical_Lutheran_Church

67   Old Exchange Building. http://www.oldexchange.org/highlights

68   Wars circa 1670. https://en.wikipedia.org/wiki/List_of_wars_1500–1799

69   Fort Moultrie. https://en.wikipedia.org/wiki/Fort_Moultrie

70   Formation of U.S. Air Force. https://www.military.com/air-force-birthday/air-force-history.html

71   Great Charleston Fire of 1838. https://www.google.com/url?sa=t&rct=j&q=

&esrc=s&source=web&cd=3&cad=rja&uact=8&ved=0ahUKEwiowb7
wj87aAhVBq1MKHQZLC6sQFggxMAI&url=https%3A%2F%2Fhistory
engine.richmond.edu%2Fepisodes%2Fview%2F3531&usg=AOvVaw
0PGxIcEoQvltLBpJHbEao_

72 Confederate Museum. https://www.confederatemuseumcharlestonsc.com
73 Ibid.
74 Charles Cotesworth Pinckney. http://www.thecharlestoncitymarket.com/main/
history
75 Karpeles Museum. http://www.gibbesmuseum.org/exhibitions/miniature-
portraits/72
76 Charleston Museum. http://www.loislaneproperties.com/resources/who-
remembers-the-old-charleston-museum
77 James Adger. http://www.scencyclopedia.org/sce/entries/adger-james/
78 Alfred Hutty. http://thejohnsoncollection.org/alfred-hutty/
79 James Sauls. Art and Artist in the South
80 Elizabeth O'Neill Verner Award. http://www.southcarolinaarts.com/verner/
81 Oscar Wilde quote. https://www.amandaholling.com/today-in-charleston
-history-oscar-wilde-comes-to-town/
82 John Locke. https://en.wikipedia.org/wiki/Fundamental_Constitutions_of
_Carolina
83 Revocation of the Edict of Nantes. https://www.museeprotestant.org/en/notice/
the-period-of-the-revocation-of-the-edict-of-nantes-1661-1700/
84 Southern Baptists. https://www.charlestonbaptist.net/history/
85 Seacoast Church. https://www.seacoast.org
86 All information above is derived from cruising the Internet. Assuming that the
information herein is factual, then this essay is thusly inured with truth.
87 National Historic Landmarks. https://theculturetrip.com/north-america/usa/
south-carolina/articles/charleston-architecture-in-8-historic-buildings/
88 Cephalonia. http://www.kefalonia-greece.com/kefalonia-history.htm
89 Thales. https://www.iep.utm.edu/thales/
90 Loss of Rice Plantations. http://halseymap.com/flash/window.asp?HMID=64
91 Old Jail. https://www.sciway.net/sc-photos/charleston-county/old-city-jail.html
92 Pink House. https://www.today.com/home/oldest-home-charleston-sale-see
-inside-t108966
93 Society of Friends. http://www.carolana.com/SC/Royal_Colony/
sc_royal_colony_quakers.html
94 Formentera. https://www.ibiza-spotlight.com/formentera/why_formentera_i.htm
95 Sinkholes. http://www.momtastic.com/webecoist/2008/08/26/incredible-

strange-amazing-sinkholes/

96   World Education. https://ourworldindata.org/quality-of-education

97   Best Countries. https://www.usnews.com/news/best-countries/overall-full-list

98   Tax Rates of Countries. Ibid.

99   Indonesia. https://www.reuters.com/article/us-usa

100 Funding Pakistan. https://www.reuters.com/article/us-usa-pakistan-aid/u-s-suspends-at-least-900-million-in-security-aid-to-pakistan-idUSKBN1ET2DX

101 Poverty in Africa. https://www.worldatlas.com/articles/poorest-countries-in-africa.html

102 Country Crime Rates. Ibid.

103 Highest Murder rates. https://list25.com/25-countries-with-the-highest-murder-rates-in-the-world/3/

104 Most Powerful Military. http://www.grinbergnews.com/powerful-militaries/

105 Ranking of Power. Ibid.

106 Ranking of Power. Ibid.

107 Quality of Life. https://www.usnews.com/news/best-countries/quality-of-life-full-list

108 World Crime Rates. https://www.usnews.com/news/best-countries/quality-of-life-full-list

Printed in the United States
By Bookmasters